Jargon

How to talk to anyone about anything.

Jargon

How to talk to anyone about anything.

Joel Homer

Illustrated by Stan Mack

𝕿imes
BOOKS

To Tobie Sullivan, my good friend

Published by TIMES BOOKS, a division of
Quadrangle/The New York Times Book Co., Inc.
Three Park Avenue, New York, N.Y. 10016

Published simultaneously in Canada by
Fitzhenry & Whiteside, Ltd., Toronto.

Copyright ©1979 by Tree Communications, Inc.
Illustrations copyright © 1979 by Stan Mack

Library of Congress Cataloging in Publication Data
Homer, Joel.
Jargon: how to talk to anyone about anything.
1. English language   Jargon. I. Title.
PE1585.H63   427.09   79-51446

ISBN 0-8129-0854-6

Manufactured in the United States of America.

Created and produced by Tree Communications, Inc.
250 Park Avenue South, New York, New York 10003

Contents

Preface

For the first several years of my life, America and I spoke the same language. Then, when I turned thirteen, something strange happened. I could no longer talk to my parents. Or to my teachers. Or, for that matter, to anyone who wasn't my approximate age. I still employed English, of course, but now it was a very particular form of English. Because conventional speech was inadequate to express the emotional and glandular chaos of adolescence, I adopted a new vocabulary to convey teen-age lyricism, teen-age profanity, teen-age nihilism—a vocabulary so teen-age, in fact, that it was virtually incomprehensible to anyone but other teen-agers. This private language gave me and my friends identity, purpose, definition. It also cut us off from adults. As alien as extraterrestrial beings, we stared at our elders across the impassable boundary of an indecipherable vernacular.

This was my introduction to the power of jargon—its power to unify and its power to estrange.

Later, home from college, I paid the ritual visit to my old high school. It was pleasant to discover that I could now communicate with my ex-instructors on a more or less equal basis. It wasn't so pleasant to discover that I could no longer communicate with the students. When I graduated, good was *boss*, bad was *nowhere*, and the grownups were *squares*. When I returned, good was *bad*, bad was *beat*, and I was as square as the grownups.

This was my introduction to the treacherous inconstancy of jargon, its quicksilver ability to change and, in changing, to date and even mock its practitioners.

During my army basic training, I was abruptly confronted with the perplexing doublespeak essential to the military establishment. Here, privates' lives were overwhelmingly public, and soldiers were instructed to *render hostile personnel inoperable* rather than to kill the enemy.

This was my introduction to the jargon of officialese, in which words march in unison, eyes forward and consciences permanently to the rear. The prime objective of these ranks upon ranks of neatly turned phrases was to camouflage reality.

I soon realized that my fellow soldiers (or *grunts*) had a language of their own, an appropriately brutal and obscene language in which war was declared *fun* (on-the-line slang for "fucking unbelievable") and all deaths, of friends or foe alike, were termed *getting wasted*.

This was my introduction to the jargon of the disenchanted—pungent words that heightened and clarified reality instead of concealing it.

Stateside again, working as a newspaper reporter, I studied those verbally adroit politicians who use yet another form of jargon to avoid, twist, shade, manipulate, or otherwise distort the truth. Quickly disillusioned, I paced restlessly back and forth across the country, absorbing the lingoes peculiar to different locales, different jobs, and new friends. As I collected the more colorful phrases and explored their definitions and derivations, I grew increasingly impressed with the power of the spoken word and increasingly curious about how jargon develops, how it changes, its various functions, and its various influences on so many of us in so many areas of our lives. No American, after all, represents only one American subgroup. A businessman is rarely a businessman only; he also may be a CB enthusiast, a self-help disciple, a military reservist. As a result, jargon often filters from one professional or social stratum to another, crosses and mates and eventually produces hybrid offspring that further complicate the language and confuse the uninitiated.

As I looked and listened around, I concluded that, for the most part, you are how you talk, and how you talk is best characterized by the jargon that you use. Essentially, jargon—or buzzwords, "in" words, slang words, cult and cant and can-do words—is restricted to a specific group. Inevitably, a once-inside term loses its exclusivity through frequent exposure to outsiders and is replaced with a more obscure substitute; the disgraced word or phrase either dies or, often, is incorporated into the language at large, whereupon it becomes institutionalized, bureaucratized and, ultimately, devitalized.

While a term is in its prime, it serves to keep secrets, to keep society segmented, and to provide adults with a socially sanctioned equivalent of pig Latin. Politicians and pimps do not talk like plumbers or producers; nor should they. In any occupation, jargon is a tool of the trade without which one cannot do business. To penetrate a particular world, it is essential to understand the language of the natives—and understanding their dramatically distinct languages is the purpose of this book.

You will find language that is remarkably colorful as well as language that is characteristically colorless. In the best, most durable jargon, form follows function, and the words heard on the streets of our cities preen and crow and swagger. The terminology of technocrats lurks and slouches and hides in pigeonholes, while the words of the sexual underworld cuddle and insinuate and seduce.

Although you'll come across words that are totally familiar, they are employed in unusual contexts or are masquerading behind new and occasionally inexplicable meanings. Conversing with Humpty Dumpty in *Through the Looking-glass,* Alice argues that *glory* does not mean a "nice knock-down argument." In return, she receives a lesson in the mutability of language and the creation of jargon.

"When I use a word," Humpty Dumpty said, in a rather scornful tone, "it means just what I want it to mean— neither more nor less."

"The question is," said Alice, "whether you can make words mean so many different things."

"The question is," said Humpty Dumpty, "which is to be master—that's all."

To enable the reader to master the jargon that distinguishes everyone from eggs to eggheads, and to comprehend their ways of doing business or avoiding business, definitions are provided for terms now in use in those areas where jargon is most prevalent and most highly developed. While you are not necessarily encouraged to employ these terms in every-day conversation, familiarity with them will enable you to inter-pret what that friendly neighborhood politico or unfriendly neighborhood teen-ager is saying (or trying not to say).

Introduction

O nce upon a time, we had to learn how to talk only
once. At the age of about six months, and to the
considerable delight of our parents, we somehow
articulated "bye-bye" and "Da-da." With that we were off and
verbally running along the course that would end with the
ability to hold a conversation. Once learned, each new word was
good for a lifetime. Or so we believed.

As things have turned out, many of us can't talk to each other
at all. The English we learned and the individual words we
mastered are often useless. They have been rudely displaced by
a variety of jargons. While the dictionary might define jargon as
being a "confused unintelligible language," it has become the
standard form of communication, at work and play, for millions
of Americans.

Although rooted in the English language, jargon takes
extraordinary liberties with our national tongue. Some versions
completely reverse the original meaning of a word. Others,
including Spook Talk (the language of spies, secret agents, and
other professional snoops), take refuge in euphemisms. Still
others, such as Political Talk, filibuster in acronyms. As if that
weren't enough, there is Helpful Talk, for those who pursue
spiritual and mental perfection, which borrows liberally from
the language of both lay and professional philosophers whose
theories profess to improve the user's heart and mind.

Since jargon is used by the initiated among the initiated, it
might seem that the rest of us are free to take it or leave it, but
this is not the case. Nowadays, jargon is unavoidable. Some
comes directly at us in the form of Political Talk; others enmesh
our every action, as in the form of Red Tape Talk. And, there's
never a let-up. Jargon users go to the same parties that we go to,
for instance, and bring their language with them. If ever the
cliché "If you can't beat 'em, join 'em" held true, it does now.
The fact is, a basic knowledge of the most common jargons will
enable you to communicate. The alternative is to revert, in
effect, to the conversational limitations of babyhood.

1
The Power Brokers

The
Power
Brokers

Big Business Talk
Political Talk
Red Tape Talk
Spook Talk
Law and Disorder Talk

As disparate as the various types of power may be, there is a common objective among those who wield it: to hang on to that power and, better yet, to expand it. Consequently, power jargons come in both defensive and offensive versions; the first is designed for public consumption and is applied as an armor; the second is for in-house use only, and employed as a weapon. In aggregate, as this section will illustrate, certainly the private jargon, and surprisingly often the public jargon, betray the true moods of the various powers that be: Big Business Talk, for instance, is bloodthirsty; Political Talk, deceiving; Red Tape Talk, evasive; Spook Talk, immoral; and Law and Disorder Talk, that not of the moralist but the pragmatist.

Insofar as the actual use of the English language is concerned, the most outrageous liberties are taken by those who are probably the best educated, namely Big Business. It can't resist, it seems, the temptation to invent extraordinary words: a *condomarinium,* for example (an amalgam of condominium and marina) means a tax shelter scheme. To *prioritize* is to rank in order of importance. Big Business Talk also borrows and steals, quite shamelessly, from various sources in its search for the right word. From the Communist Party comes *apparatchik* (originally used to describe a junior Party member, it now means a junior executive). From the French military comes *rebarbative* (literally, "beard to beard" but now meaning an acrimonious business confrontation); from the Pueblo Indians comes *kiva* (a sacred ceremonial chamber, now the executive suite).

Politicians also invent words (*autarky*, meaning a country that is capable of sustaining itself economically, for example). And they delve into all-Americanisms, adapting what they find to get their point across. A *barnburner*, for example, is a political renegade who puts principle above party. (If a *barnburner* is called in by his peers in an effort to pull him back into line, the meeting is called a *board of education*.) *Mom and Pop Meets* are gathering where the issue of birth control is likely to be raised. To *cow-waddle* is to attempt to head off passage of new legislation by the tactic of going through the voting process as slowly as possible, a kind of ambulatory filibuster.

When it comes to delaying tactics, of course, nobody can compete with bureaucrats. Red Tape Talk is replete with examples, the most fitting of which is *bureaucratization*, which means the process of dividing and then redividing authority. This is practiced to such an extent that even simple jobs don't get done and simple decisions are never made. It's a very common tactic, because bureaucrats are, by definition, really loath to do or even say anything that they can be held responsible for. Red Tape Talk for waffle is *bafflegab*.

The mastery of *bafflegab* generally guarantees that the bureaucrat will be able to enjoy a *ceegee* (cradle-to-grave) lifetime career as a government employee, particularly if he or she manages to *residuate*, or maintain a low profile. Those with high profiles risk ending up as *postles*, or fired. (The word is a bastardization of a Latin word describing exiles.)

A not dissimilar sense of *bafflegab* spills over into Spook Talk. Words like *destabilize* (to overthrow a foreign government) and *minus advantage* (the result of an operation that leaves things in a worse condition than they were before) have the distinct ring of the bureaucrat. Other Spook Talk, however, is far more scary— largely because it sounds innocent or, worse, downright laudable. *Botanicals,* for instance, are organic drugs that can wipe out a nation's livestock (and, though of relatively minor importance, cause national hairlessness). *Nod out* is the end result of lethal poison that cannot be detected in an autopsy. *Motivation* means blackmail. *Human ecology* means brainwashing.

The Power Brokers

Big Business Talk

(the) abreaction route	In psychology, *abreaction* is the discharge of tension in the presence of the analyst; in big business, *abreaction route* describes the channels provided by management to allow employees to harmlessly blow off steam and to work out their frustrations without disrupting the status quo. (One of the most extreme examples of such a channel is the gym facilities a certain Japanese firm has provided for its staff. On each punching bag has been pasted a photograph of the firm's president.) Because the *abreaction route* is usually designed to lull workers into placidity rather than to truly humanize working conditions, it's also called *cow sociology, stroke sessions,* and *Dr. Spocking the help.*
ACES	Acronym for Authoritarian Conscience Employees. According to Dr. Erich Fromm, the authoritarian conscience is internalized fear of authority, which makes for a fearful and obedient approach toward one's job. According to most personnel departments, people burdened with such consciences make ideal employees, as in "I recommend hiring Jones for this position. He's ACES all the way—no complaints about overtime, no demands for raises, and no undermining of authority."
adhocracy	Term first coined by futurologist Alvin Toffler to describe the new form of task-force management that, unlike traditional organizations, is created for short-term projects.
administralia	The (very crowded) room at the top, inhabited by managers, vice-presidents, and executives of all shapes and sizes, that is the controlling force in the world of big business.

anationals

Companies so large, spread out, and dominating, that they have no real homeland.

apparatchik

Lower-echelon staff, *e.g.*, a junior executive or an administrative assistant. The word *apparatchik* was originally created by the Russians to describe young members of the Communist Party System.

asthenic gameplan

Asthenic describes a person suffering from fear, loss of general mental functions, and an inability to act decisively. *Gameplan* is a much-loved phrase among big business types, probably because its sportslike connotations disguise the often Machiavellian, often cruel practices it describes. The *asthenic gameplan* is any method employed by a businessman to intimidate a subordinate (most common), a superior (least common), or a rival in line for the same job promotion.

BB's

Barn Burners: people who are unusually skilled at getting their work done.

blizzard wizard

A particularly choice accolade awarded to only the very best sales promoters. Named in honor of Stanley Arnold, whose family owned a supermarket chain in Ohio. When, one winter, a blizzard prevented any customers from visiting the supermarkets for several days, Mr. Arnold first ordered all 15 stores closed, and then directed the employees to go out into the parking lots and make snowballs. He next arranged for the snowballs, 7,000 in all, to be stored in deep-freezers until the following summer, when they were each packed in a cellophane bag and handed out to every 200th customer. So successful was this idea that the Ohio Police Department had to be called out to handle the enormous crowds. The supermarkets more than made up their losses, the happy customers received a handful of slush, and Stanley Arnold became famous throughout the business world.

blobocracy

Fiercely sardonic word devised to characterize those corporations that have become too fat and complacent to change with the times.

candle

To inspect; to examine; an outsider's investigation of the inner workings of an organization. As in "The Health Department *candled* our factory yesterday." The word is derived from the old-time procedure of inspecting eggs for quality by placing a candle behind them.

cerebral conclave

A description of the most popular of all business practices—except, that is, turning a profit—the staff conference. Also, the *groupthink, brainstorming,* and *a meeting of the medullae.*

chapel meeting

Labor slang for a union meeting deliberately called during work hours, thus legally creating a job slowdown. (In addition to its religious usage, the word "chapel" was employed to describe the 17th-century English Guild of Printers.)

coal and ice

The basic operating theory upon which all successful firms rest: In winter you sell coal; in the summer you sell ice. "Let's stick to the *coal and ice*" means "Let's stay with the basics and not get involved in any more elaborate plans."

cocktail party hangover	Oppressive condition suffered by a business-man forced to choose advice from one of many vociferous consultants. When the businessman must choose one from many options, he's said to be suffering from a *candy store stomachache.*
cold shower time	"It's *cold shower time,*" like its predecessor "back to the drawing board," is a buzzphrase for "our first plan didn't work so we have to start all over again." In those lofty aeries where the corporate heads perch, this is also referred to as *manually excavating the artifacts.*
condomarinium	First coined as a humorous reference to land-based yachts (combining the two expressions, "condominium" and "marina"); nowadays, a very serious reference to any tax-shelter scheme.
consloperators	*Conglomerates* are widely diversified corporations; *congloperators* are the heads of conglomerates; therefore, it stands to reason that *consloperators* are conglomerate presidents either incompetent or overly greedy.
contrameritocracy	A word nearly impossible to say without stuttering, *contrameritocracy* is any organized group opposed to any other organized group that's in a ruling or power position.
cream at the top	Perks (that is, the perquisite benefits offered to executive personnel). Like cream in the milk, most company benefits rise to the top.
(the) creep veep	Every efficient corporation has one vaguely titled vice-president whose real job is to cut all the deadwoods—departments, staff, etc.—

that are monkey wrenches in the profit-making machinery. The *creep veep* is not particularly popular, as evidenced by his nickname, but he is essential. Also called, to his face, the somewhat more flattering term, *sockdologer* (from *doxology,* now dated business lingo for anything that settles a problem in a direct and decisive manner).

deal stream Derisive term for the endless line of would-be entrepreneurs streaming through the typical manager's office, each with large deals and little funding.

dedomiciling Buzztalk for moving a company from one state to another state in which there are fewer limitations (read: fewer taxes placed on its operations). Also used by business executives to describe a marital separation or divorce: "Yes, Pat and I are now in the process of *dedomiciling.*" If the marriage is saved, the executive announces his return to marital bliss with the phrase, *re-dedomiciling.*

executive eatery The trough offered by corporations to highly rated but still-hungry executives as an incentive to join the team. The typical bill of fare includes deferred bonus plans, stock options, and various perks. Also, *the compensation café.*

executive fallout When a company merges with a conglomerate, many of the original executives end up on the unemployment line. *Executive fallout* is a polite replacement for "purge."

externalizing internals Executive parlance for taking company policy and making it your own personal policy, one of the best ways to climb up the rickety corporate ladder. (Another, more explicit, term for this process would be "brown-nosing.") Never to be confused with *internalizing the externals,* an entirely different concept based on the practice of anticipating the unexpected in policy-planning.

4F   The less than healthy condition of every new business enterprise, *i.e.,* no Funds, no Fringes, no Facilities, and (unless the enterprise is particularly well-managed) no Future.

fratority   Traditionally, Ivy League graduates have dominated the top-executive ranks; thus, "The Gray-Flannel Fraternity." Women's liberation has now made that phrase obsolete. Fraternity has wed sorority, and their offspring is *fratority.*

the Fribbish scale   Mr. Fribbish is, in big business mythology, the black-shoes-with-brown-suit executive unburdened by propriety, manners, or simple good taste. *The Fribbish scale* is a not always humorous way to rate personnel. An office manager who wears checkered suits, for instance, receives a *Fribbish 3* rating. A vice-president who puts a "Jokes for the John" book in the executive washroom earns a *Fribbish 6.* The sales manager who hires a personal secretary who is attractive but incompetent has won a *Fribbish 10* (and, most likely, an eventual pink slip).

fungible   Originally a legal term meaning something that can be satisfactorily used to replace something else (*e.g.,* an obligation to pay money can be cleared by paying the equivalent in stocks);

now, business lingo for a Renaissance-type employee who can be moved from one task to another without any diminishment of his skills. The *Fungible Cowboy,* like the Lone Ranger, is a priceless commodity on anyone's range.

gazumphing   Charming description—taken from the Yiddish *gezumph* (which means a pinch on the cheek)—of the uncharming practice of boosting the price of an item (often a house) after the deal has already been made.

Got   One who's in a position of power, success, comfort. As in "I'm happy in my life. I guess you could say that I'm a *Got." Antigot* is the revolutionary out to topple the establishment; *Poligot* is the establishment advocate who's gotten plenty but who wants plenty more; *No-got* is both self-explanatory and—for most of us, anyway—all too familiar.

hi-bye boss   One of the least difficult, and also least productive abreaction channels an employer can set up is to have an "open-door" policy. This means that every worker gets a doubtful morale-booster of his boss greeting him each time he passes the office, and also the *Hi-Bye Boss* gets a brand-new way to waste a lot of time.

(to) grayhair it   When stuck on a problem, a young executive may choose to *grayhair it;* that is, he may approach an older, wiser, and grayer head for help.

honglomerates   Pun combining conglomerate and Hong Kong, invented by *The London Economist* to define those multiple firms that are centered in the Far East.

HPV

When one considers what these initials stand for, namely the Holocyclatic Point of View, it's easy to see why the abbreviated form has prevailed. *Holocyclate,* from the Greek, means a panoramic consideration of a situation. The *HPV*—that is, the objective viewpoint—is the only way in which a good business manager approaches problems and/or proposed actions; the *APV*—that is, the Administrative Point of View—is a more subjective, and thus more limited, consideration that never strays beyond the corporate frame of reference. "What's good for Business is good for America" is the ultimate (and the ultimately fatal) *APV* slogan.

intermodalist

The corporate lexicon is crowded with various imposing titles of rank; all are filled with sound and fury, all but a few signify nothing much to speak of. An *intermodalist,* for example, is simply the worker who deals with the forwarding of freight from his company. In other, less-embellished words, a mail clerk.

jets

A *jet* is an employee who has grown too big for his gray-flannel suit; that is, a hotshot whose opinion of himself is higher than his opinion of the company. One wit has suggested that considering the rapid attrition rate, *jet* is actually an acronym for "Jettisoned Employee in Training."

job inaction

Yet another jokey in-phrase. This one is a reasonably appropriate reaction to the "job action," that union-sanctioned strategy in which workers are directed to deliberately slow down their rate of production.

kilobucks   The American Dream: one million dollars, after taxes.

KITA   Kick In The Ass. A system of employee-motivation developed by the Harvard School of Business, the *KITA* has two possible applications: the positive kick, which induces employees to motivate themselves to do a better job; and the negative kick, which eventually, if too often used, induces employees to *find* a better job. Recently, however, a few of the more radicalized Harvard Business School members have devised an alternate theory, called the *POTB* (Pat On The Butt), which suggests that employees are human enough to need a little active encouragement now and then.

kiva   Pueblo Indian word for the sacred ceremonial chamber of the tribal mystic. Adapted by the big chiefs of commerce as a buzzword describing the executive suites in which all major business decisions are made. Hotels have been competing for the patronage of corporate leaders by setting up special units that include conference rooms along with the more standard bedroom/sitting room/bath. The Hilton chain has recently begun advertising such units as "VIP kivas."

label Mabels   Mabel is the joy of big business; the perfect consumer, she buys on the basis of a label rather than the contents of a commodity. *Label*

Mabels, however, have no place on the payroll of a company that wants creative—not emotional—thinking. The *label Mabel* is an executive ruled by a prejudiced heart instead of an objective brain.

Martian approach

Robert Townsend, who steered Avis Rent-A-Car to success, explains: "In solving a complex problem, pretend that you are a Martian. Assume that you understand everything about Man and his society—except what has been done in the past by other companies in your industry to solve this particular problem."

maximax

If a company, weighing a variety of options, chooses to go with the one that has both the biggest potential pay-off and also the biggest potential disaster, said company has made a *maximax* decision (that is, it has put all its chips on one roll of the dice). If, conversely, the company plays it safe with a less profitable—but less risky—option, it has made a *minimax* decision. Finally, if the company erroneously selects the option which has the least to gain and the most to lose, it has made a *maximin* decision. Also known as the *risk reward ratio.*

melons

Jargon for extra dividends. Profits are the fertilizer; *melons* are the fruit. As in "Good news, stockholders. There'll be *melons* in your garden this year."

monospony

A business trader who is the only buyer of a certain commodity—cuff links, say—in his area of operations is said to be running a *monospony.*

morphological analysis	Developed by Dr. Fritz Swicky, this is currently the preferred method of systematized problem-solving. First, the manager lists all possible variables to the problem; next, he places all the possible variables of the variables; then, he places all the variables in a 3-dimensional cardboard box with window cutouts. In this manner, the manager supposedly can mix and match various solutions simultaneously, thus achieving an overview of the problem.
now-wows	Nomenclature reserved for that element of the executive rank and file constantly urging the abolishment of the entrenched management's rules and strictures.
officered	Persuasive buzzword for an executive's not-so-innocent ascendancy in his company. As in "Brown's *officered* himself from the stockroom to a vice-presidency in less than two years."
paripotence	A compromise; more specifically, coming to terms with the difference between one's reach and one's grasp. A combination of omnipotence and impotence, the *paripotent* businessman has learned to enjoy his advantages and has also reconciled himself to his limitations.
people plucker	An executive recruiter. *People plucker* seems to be replacing the less euphemistic—and more aggressive—"headhunter" to describe those firms that specialize in seducing top-notch employees away from one company to another.
polling the room	Asking subordinates what they think of a particular proposal; *polling the nabs* is asking

your family and friends; *polling the hornrims* is referring the proposal to the staff intellectuals; *polling the wiz* is engaging a computer to reach the proper decision for you.

poweradoxical
Buzzword employed by managers and executives who have been given power without the means to put that power into effective use. "It's not that I'm ungrateful, sir, but don't you think putting me in charge of Market Research, especially when there's no Market Research Department, is a bit *poweradoxical?*"

prioritize
To rank, in an ascending order, the goals of a company's policy is to "*prioritize* the issues at hand."

profundicator
Any executive who has a marked talent for translating the simplest proposal into the most complicated language. Also known as a *synomaniac* ("syno" being short for synonym).

pseudologia phantastica
If either a subordinate or an equal is caught in a lie, he's—well—lying. If it's either an equal with clout or a superior, he's indulging in some harmless *pseudologia phantastica*.

psychic compensation
Any career benefit that lacks monetary value. When your boss congratulates you on a job well done without offering you anything more substantial than praise, you've just been the recipient of some *psychic compensation*.

putteristics
There are executives who waste time, and then there are executives who've transformed wasting time into a precise science. The latter are known as master *putteristics*.

rebarbative	A word derived from a French military phrase that literally means "beard to beard," that is used to characterize an unpleasant business confrontation.
repotting	When an executive chooses to leave his job and accept employment elsewhere, he's *repotting* himself.
rhocrematics	A buzzword—used only by corporate heads—to describe the basic process of transforming raw materials into consumer-acceptable products.
riding shotgun	In the modern conference room, a proposal is made by two colleagues: one drives home the basic facts, the other—*riding shotgun*—fields all the questions.
satisficer	A co-joining of satisfy and suffice, a *satisficer* proposal is a deal that is sufficient but not thoroughly satisfactory.
space cadets	Young executives who consider things other than straight company profits in mapping their business strategies. Business versions of *eco-freaks;* those concerned with environmental and other quality-of-life issues.
stratified cluster probability	The carefully layered data, gathered from polls, that determine the probability of the results of business ventures.
subanoncoccygeal plumbism	Rough translation: "Too much lead in one's pants." Diagnosis of malingering executives who continually take off sick days for no other reason than laziness.

synergistic effects of disparate affiliates Tongue-twister that means nothing more than "Two heads are better than one."

TIT Totally Integrated Transaction; that is, a job offer complete with all possible compensation benefits. If a male potential employee is offered a position "with big *TITS*," he should not get confused (or overly excited). All it means is that the company is willing to provide him with generous benefits.

titlewave The *Wall Street Journal* invented this clever catchphrase to describe the typical executive shakeup, in which staff personnel are promoted, shifted, or fired *en masse*.

uppity In any other area, being called *uppity* would be, at best, a mild reproof. In big business, however, the term is used admiringly to characterize an executive skilled in the art of one-upmanship.

wooden stake To permanently shelve an idea, proposal, or policy, as in "Let's *wooden stake* this." Only the highest of high-echelon executives are in a position to use this term.

X theory The controlling principle of authoritarian-oriented corporate heads who are dedicated to the principle of absolute control over their employees. The term was invented by business expert Douglas McGregor to define the robber-baron mentality prevalent among 19th-century American business tycoons.

The Power Brokers
Political Talk

(the) AAA club
The triple A stands for Accommodation, Accountability, and Appeasement, three buzzwords that describe, respectively, a willingness to compromise, a commitment to various pressure groups, and an ability to spread oil over troubled waters. Any congressman or congresswoman who consistently displays these attributes is said to be a member in good standing of the *AAA club*.

Aesop's fables
White House slang for the daily press briefing. Aesop, a Greek slave, prudently concealed his social and political messages within seemingly innocuous fairytales. The parallel, at least for anyone who's ever sat through a Presidential briefing, is self-explanatory.

alarmists
The first of the three basic derogatory terms used to dismiss the caviling of a political opponent. The term *alarmist* is reserved for those who point out possible problems inherent in a policy; *defeatists* is used to characterize those who question the policy's results; and *extremists* is used for those who encounter the policy with a contrasting policy of their own.

(the) alligator principle
Asked how he could concentrate on "winning" the war in Vietnam while protesters paraded back and forth beneath his windows, President Lyndon Baines Johnson replied, "When you're up to your ass in alligators, don't forget your job is to drain the swamp."

(going) ape
Most public officials reach a point in their careers when, through either sincere belief or cynical reassessment of their power, they decide to abandon their own party line. Hence,

the acronym *ape* for "above political expediencies" has come into use. For example, in 1971, *The New York Times* praised Senator Sam Ervin for "moving beyond politics into statesmanship"; among his colleagues, however, this move was described as "Senator Sam going *ape*."

autarkic   An up-to-date buzzword for an economically feasible government plan; also, in noun form, *autarky,* which is employed to identify any nation capable of economic self-sufficiency.

back channel   Once a euphemism, exclusive to the CIA, for secret communication networks; now a no longer hush-hush expression that describes any unofficial routing of information: a private phone conversation between diplomats of two different nations, for instance, is called a *back-channel chat.*

balkanization   In modern usage, refers to the process in which a nation is given military support only with the understanding that it will eventually be prepared to fight its own battles by itself. In the Sixties, the phrase for this process was Vietnamization; given its ineffectiveness, it was replaced by the term *balkanization.*

ballot security   Electioneering code word indicating a safe lead in the voter polls.

bap   *Bap* (rhymes with "zap") is an abbreviation for Bay of Pigs, which was and is viewed as the single greatest fiasco of the Kennedy Administration. The word now has a broader frame of reference, covering any disastrous consequence of a political move, as in "My stand on nuclear reactors really *bapped* me with the folks back home."

barnburners

Euphemism for *renegades,* itself a euphemism for a member of one's own party who is willing to risk total loss in pursuit of an ideal, a principle, or a particular personal goal. The term is derived from an old saw which admonishes, "Don't burn down the barn to kill the mice."

beercan player

In sports, the *beercan player* is an athlete who would rather sit on the bench than participate on the field; in politics, it's a contemptuous label for any politician reluctant to enter the fray.

bircher

Once a member of the right-wing reactionary John Birch Club; now a member of any extremist group, whether it be right-wing or left-wing or just off-the-wall. Also known as *crazies, nuts and kooks, the lunatic fringe,* and *little old ladies in tennis shoes.*

birdwatchers

In public, politicos call them *environmentalists* and *concerned citizens.* In private, they're called *birdwatchers* and *eco-nuts.*

bite the bullet

Not a new phrase but—thanks to its current widespread use—one worth noting here. There are two distinct meanings: if a politician announces that he's about to *bite the bullet,* he simply means he's making a decision; if, however, the same politician declares that *we* (*i.e.,* the voters) have to do the biting, he means that his decision is going to adversely affect us (*e.g.,* a tax increase) and, too, that he hopes we'll accept our burden stoically and not blame him for so saddling us.

Black Plague   A time-honored political ploy is to plant unfounded (and untraceable) rumors about your opponent. This is known as spreading the *Black Plague*. Also, *dirty tricks, nut-cracking*, and *rat-fucking*.

Board of Education   Whenever it's deemed necessary, the most influential members of the House of Representatives arrange to hold a meeting with some of their more maverick-styled junior colleagues. During the course of this informal assemblage, the young rebels are plied with liquor, calmed with flattery, and reminded—gently— of where the real power lies. The practice is now practiced in local precincts; today, any senior group of politicians convened to remind their younger and more headstrong partners about keeping in line is known as a *Board of Education*.

bomfog   Any speech heavy on bombastic rhetoric and light on true substance. *Bomfog* is a wonderfully pointed acronym for Brotherhood of Man, Fatherhood of God, a meaningless catchphrase much used by the late Nelson Rockefeller.

camp   Acronym for Campaign Promises, as in "We've got to come up with a new *camp* for our candidate." The connection with the more common definition of the word (that is, anything so far out of fashion that it is a fashionable joke) is as inadvertent as it is accurate.

cannibalism   A usually negative word for inter-party dispute. The losing side of the argument will claim to have been "attacked by the cannibals"; the winning side, however, will claim to have "broadened our power base."

chips   Any concession offered to sweeten the passage of a legislative bill is regarded to be a bargaining *chip*. Such *chips* are the basis for most political wheeling and dealing.

Christmas-tree   In the *Wall Street Journal,* reporter Alan Otten defined it thus: "On Capitol Hill, the practice of tagging a host of special-interest amendments to a popular bill is known as '*Christmas-treeing*' that bill."

classified at birth   Nomenclature for information so secret that it's thus classified the very moment the information is first gathered.

controversial   Private code word used in public announcements to inform one's colleagues of a policy position without having to reveal it to the outside world. "I have not yet decided how I will act on this *controversial* issue" means, on the contrary, "I've already decided *against* this issue but I'm not yet willing to put my opposition on the record."

cowwaddle   The filibuster is a political attempt to delay passage of legislation by constant talking. The *cowwaddle* is also an attempt to delay passage, this time by going through the voting process as slowly as possible. The word was first used to describe the painfully slow progress of a herd of reluctant cattle.

creeping	A derogatory adjective employed to indicate a political concept that spreads stealthily, without fanfare or public attention.
Cro-Magnon	Half-affectionate, half not-so-affectionate way of characterizing the older, more opinionated, and usually rock-ribbed conservative elements in Congress. Also, *the Old Boys, the Old Pros, the Old Soldiers, the Old Guard, the Old Fogies,* and *the League of Dinosaurs.*
dee que	That is, Deniability Quotient. "What's the *dee que* on this position?" can be translated as "If I make this decision, how much of the responsibility can I safely deny to the public?"
deliberate speed	A convenient phrase that promises a great deal without having to deliver much of anything. Harassed by outraged voters on an issue he intends to take absolutely no action upon, the world-wise politician can lean back in his chair, purse his lips thoughtfully, and reply, "I'm cognizant of the problem, and let me assure you that I'm moving with all *deliberate speed* to correct it." *Deliberate speed* is an oxymoron (*e.g.,* "cruel kindness") that can—and often does—actually describe the approximate travel rate of a glacier.
demarche	Technically, diplomatic slang for any move that can be regarded as a step forward in international tactics. Lately, however, *demarche* is being used by many politicians as a substitute for the less popular "détente."
deucing	A sudden inflation increase equaling at least a ten percent jump. Also *double-digiting.*

dippers A deliberately abstruse euphemism for government employees (most typically retired military officers with pension benefits) who enjoy at least two tax-supported incomes.

disinformation In the world of politics, there are many interesting distinctions between truth and lie. *Disinformation* is one: a piece of news that itself is true but that leads the listener to draw false conclusions. "I do not choose to run," for example, does not mean "I don't want to run"; in fact, it probably means "No one's asked me to run." Nevertheless, the speaker has *disinformed* his audience of his true intentions.

drab An acronym for "Doesn't Rock Any Boats," the *drab* is a title awarded to those politicians who don't believe in making waves.

Easy I's Easy Identification; that is, those immediately recognizable features or eccentricities—FDR's cigarette holder, for instance, or Jimmy Carter's teeth—that identify a candidate to the public.

Everest committee Humorist Will Rogers once wrote, "I hear tell Congress is a mite concerned with its members' tendency to form a committee at the drop of a hat. But everything's all right now. Congress has just announced it's forming a committee to investigate." Capitol Hill has a reputation for creating problems and then creating groups to solve these problems. The *Everest committee* is any Congressional team organized to study something just because, like Mount Everest, "it's there."

eyeballing	The kind of situation all diplomats dread: the direct confrontation. The term was used during the Cuban Missile Crisis, when then-Secretary of State Dean Rusk reported, "We're eyeball to eyeball, and I think the other fellow just blinked." An ability to *eyeball* is to show grace and constructive force while under pressure; in the Cold War, this was called *brinkmanship*.
factrips	A *factrip* is a sincere attempt on a politician's part to gather information at the source. Never to be confused with a *fact-finding trip,* which is an overseas vacation taken by a politician at the expense of the taxpayer.
family jewels	Considering its sober-sided and iron-jawed public image, the FBI displayed a surprising levity when it acknowledged that J. Edgar Hoover's personal files were known within the department as the *family jewels.* Supposedly, Hoover had kept careful records of America's politicians—including all their sexual *faux pas*—for several decades.
FAT	Flush And True. "I've got some *fat* people behind me" doesn't refer to the support of Weight Watchers but rather to the kind of backer—both wealthy and loyal—that every elective official wants on his team. Also, *fat cat.*
(putting his) feet to the fire	Deceptively comfy euphemism that really means applying political pressure to someone in order to compel him to cooperate with one's own aims.
flaps down	Derived from an old-time aviation term for a frightened pilot who tends to fly close to the

ground. A public official with his *flaps down* is someone who—temporarily, at least—is trying to keep a very low profile. As in "Ever since he was criticized on the ERA vote, the Senator's kept his door locked, his mouth shut, and his *flaps* well *down*."

fluttering
Fluttering the help is code for submitting your own people to a lie-detector test (or its equivalent). Most likely named after the flutter ing action of the needle each time a subject strapped to the machine tells a lie.

fuzzistics
The science of fuzzy thinking. Anyone can be vague; to be *deliberately* vague, however, requires much practice, training, and native skill. A *fuzzistic* official is a politician well-schooled in all methods of fielding and dodging the great burning issues of his (and our) times.

going toes up
A politico who's just declared bankruptcy, been slapped in public by a go-go dancer from the Whiskey Lounge, or—worst of all—lost his bid for re-election is *going toes up* down the tubes. Also, *belly-up* (as in the floating position of a dead fish).

going to POO
POO means "Program Zero Zero," astronaut lingo for clear the on-board computer and feed new data into it. If a politician says he has to *go to POO*, he'll get back to you (or to your question) after he's studied it more.

half breeds
A not very flattering nomenclature for supporters who do not belong to the supportee's political party. (*Non*-supporters who belong to

the correct party are described as "renegades off the reservation").

hardboiled eggheads

Originally, of course, *egghead* was a risible way of describing intellectuals. Nowadays, however, intellectuals are back in political and public favor. At least, *hardboiled* (that is, tough-minded) *eggheads* are; softer-dispositioned thinkers, however, are still condemned as *scrambled eggheads.*

Humpty Dumpty

Gobbledygook. Doubletalk. Half-truths, half-lies, and disinformation. When a speech is called *Humpty Dumpty,* it's filled to the brim with flapdoodle signifying nothing. When a speaker is called *Humpty Dumpty*—and by the way, this is an affectionate, even complimentary label—he is a master of fuzzistics. The phrase may be traced back to the original egghead himself, who, in Lewis Carroll's *Through the Looking-glass,* explains his own theory of linguistics: " 'When I use a word,' Humpty Dumpty said, in a rather scornful tone, 'it means just what I choose it to mean.' "

hunting license

James Bond has a license to kill. Certain heavyweight officials, by virtue of seniority or executive-branch connections or personal power, also have a license to kill—to kill bills, proposals, and careers, too. As in "You can mock the Deputy Mayor. You can bait the Press Secretary. But don't mess with the Sanitation Commissioner—he has a *hunting license.*"

ICE

Incidental Company Expenses; a catchall phrase used by many businesses to conceal various perks and paddings of the old expense account. This is the first budget item the IRS scrutinizes when its suspicions are aroused. The word, in its verb form, has now crossed the hall into the legislative department. "Let's *ICE* this bastard" is Congressional jargon for "Let's see if we can get the goods on this guy."

iceberg politics   A statesman who conducts two-thirds of his business out of sight of the public eye is engaging in *iceberg politics.*

inadvertent criticality   Buzzphrase for a serious mistake. "The Administration regrets to announce an *inadvertent criticality* arising from its oil-shortage policy" is a convoluted way of saying "We really screwed up the oil problem this time."

interdictment   This is a very civilized word that conceals a particularly elaborate form of in-fighting among government representatives. *Interdicting* means to stop, at any cost, either a legislative bill or legislator from succeeding. The filibuster, the cloakroom manipulations, the gossip and innuendo—all are considered fair means of *interdictment.*

(the) junior angel lobby   A senator, who will remain unnamed here, was driven to distraction by a group of Gray Panthers objecting to such figurative labels as *senior citizens* and *golden oldies.* "Hell," the senator finally shouted to a trusted staff member, "if they don't like being called golden agers, let's call 'em junior angels!" An aide promptly passed on his employer's indiscretion to everyone on Capitol Hill, where American citizens over 60 are now known by the term. As the average age of senators is, at last count, over 60, it has yet to be determined whether calling the elderly *junior angels* is a bit of Congressional impudence or a large chunk of wishful thinking.

keeping the church in the middle of the village

In most European towns, the church stands in the central square, thus symbolizing its power and stability in society. Sometimes, in the heat of the moment, a political battle gets out of control and threatens not just the combatants but their parties as well. At this point, a cooler head will utter the admonishment, "Fight if you must, but *keep the church in the middle of the village.*" In other words, Don't mess with the system itself.

links

Minor tokens or gifts handed out by a President to his various supporters. The term *links* contains two puns: the gifts not only link the Chief Executive to grateful recipients, but will also often come in the form of cuff links bearing the Presidential Seal. Lyndon Johnson was noted for his "Presidential" electric toothbrushes.

log cabin

Ever since Benjamin Harrison handed out small duplicates of the rough-planked house in which he was born, the log cabin has played an important part in campaigning for office. Today, of course, it takes money to run; even so, many a prospective candidate *log cabins* it— that is, tries to identify himself with the common man. (Any elective hopeful, particularly a rich one, who overdoes the common-touch routine is accused of suffering from "logorrhea.")

lulu	*Lulu* is based on "in lieu of" itemized expenses and is a flat sum paid to legislators and public officials.
Metro American	First, *Middle America;* then *The Silent Majority;* now, *Metro American.* No matter how you say it, however, it still remains the much-put-upon middle-class United States voter.
milk for the Hottentots	This unique phrase came out of a 1942 speech made by Vice President Henry Wallace in which he pledged that everyone in the world would someday have the privilege of drinking a quart of milk a day. Used against Wallace by his conservative foes, the phrase was distorted to *milk for the Hottentots,* and the phrase still exists today. A few years ago, Herman Kahn cited four "typical," that is, ideal rather than practical, U.S. foreign policies: Rule of Law, just and lasting peace, four freedoms, and *milk for the Hottentots.*
Mom & Pop meets	Generic term for any political meeting in which birth-control is the main topic of discussion. *Mom* is an acronym for Memos on Marriage, *Pop* stands for Policy on Population.
Nervenkrieg	A German word for "psychological warfare," widely used by the more sophisticated political strategists in this country. An attack on the morals of an opponent is considered to be a *Nervenkrieg;* likewise, scare tactics, emotional appeals, and the television-ad campaign blitz.
nickel and diming	In business parlance, to *nickel and dime* is to keep track of every expenditure, no matter

how small; in political lingo, it means that a candidate is willing to personally appeal to every delegate, no matter how small his voting bloc.

paper the file

Papering the file is a government buzzphrase describing the old but ever popular ploy of inserting a memo in the files that passes blame from yourself to someone—anyone—else (two similar moves are *sanitizing the file* or *signing off the files,* or talking an unwary superior into cosigning the memo and thus into sharing the blame).

photops

Abbreviated form of *photo opportunity, i.e.,* any event in which a politicking candidate can be assured of getting his picture taken.

povertycrat

Civil servant who earns his keep working in a government anti-poverty program.

quagmire

A buzzword verb describing a messy entanglement in another country's affairs, as in "We really *quagmired* our troops in Vietnam."

rain dance

A political dinner, reception, or assemblage of any kind that is heavy on pomp and light on circumstance, *i.e.,* a ceremonial event of little practical consequence.

raw meat

When, in the course of an otherwise rational and well-reasoned speech, the guest of honor begins to shout and wave his hands about, he is throwing out *raw meat* to his audience. Any inflammatory statement or gesture that plays to the listeners' emotions can be included in this definition.

rhinestone vocabulary	The astute professional speechwriter will always try to include a few phrases germane to the particular group his boss is planning on addressing. (If it's a political rally for farmers, say, the speech will be peppered with "what's good for the crops is good for the nation" and "let us plow together.")
ride-out	In the late Fifties and early Sixties, Southern segregationists tried to solve the black problem by offering them one-way transportation to all points north. The few blacks who accepted the deal were called *ride-outs*. Today, the *ride-out* is a politician of any color who's committed a not yet publicly revealed blunder and has been persuaded to quietly resign rather than tarnish his (and his party's) name. Although there's no fixed price, his reward for going peacefully is usually considered more substantial than a bus ticket.
riffed	RIF is an acronym for "Reduction in Force," most commonly used when being fired during a change in administration. "I've been *riffed*" means "Now that the political power has transferred hands, someone in the new group's favor has replaced me." It should be noted that *rif* has become so common a word that Webster's now defines it as an appropriate term for being removed from any line of work.
SASS	Salami Tactics; *i.e.*, a political strategy in which one's position is entrenched and one's power is gathered slice by careful slice. Any politician particularly gifted at such tactics is thus honored by being called *sassy*.

scissor up

Any opinion or judgment developed by piecing together the opinions and judgments of others has been *scissored up, i.e.,* arranged without any original input or creativity.

snow threshold

A gullible, easily bullied, or credulous politician is said, contemptuously, to have a low *snow threshold.* Any official so hampered is not long for the public arena.

sound hound

Some politicos are voracious readers; others—the *sound hounds*—prefer to gather information from television news shows, personal reports, and private conversations.

terminological inexactitude

No politician lies; instead, at the very worst, he has indulged in a little *terminological inexactitude.*

tissue

Very private code word for "trivial issue." At the center of all political campaigning is the need to find a theme, any theme, that can bring the voters into the fold. Sometimes, this is a *gut issue, i.e.,* a genuinely important concern; sometimes, though, when there are no gut issues at hand, the candidate must make do with a *tissue, i.e.,* an impossible solution to an implausible problem.

unk-unks

Space-age talk for the *unknown* unknowns, those mysteries that have yet to be discovered, let alone explained. Government talk for those variables not plotted into the political game plan. As in "Senator Muskie had the nomination all sewed up, and then he was hit by the New Hampshire *unk-unks.*"

The Power Brokers

Red Tape Talk

acabu

Acronym for Academic Bureaucratic; also, *manacrat* for Management Bureaucrat, *milicrat* for Military Bureaucrat, and *polibu* for Political Bureaucrat. All of them, of course, are *probus* (pronounced "prō boos"), that is, Professional Bureaucrats. Regardless of the various professions they may represent, however, *probus* share several common character traits: a cautious demeanor, a love for doubletalk, and a well-protected derrière.

acceptable

As in "acceptable unemployment," "acceptable poverty," etc. Currently, this is the most popular adjective in the bureaucratic vocabulary. *Acceptable* within this context can be translated to mean "Yes, some people are going to get hurt, but thank God it won't be us."

alarmist

In-ranks condemnation of anyone who threatens to make trouble. "All right, so our department's temporarily misplaced a measly hundred thousand dollars in war-widows' pension benefits. That's no reason to get excited. You wouldn't want me to spread the word that you're an *alarmist,* would you?"

ancillary civil agencies for supportive discipline

Acabu lingo for the group to call (police) when, for example, the students are rioting in the cafeteria. In other words, "Call the cops!"

anodiplosis

Favorite rhetorical device of top-level bureaucrats in which the last word of a sentence is used to begin the next sentence. This is clever. Clever because it encourages boredom. Boredom leads to inattention. Inattention is the goal of every probu. Every probu's goal is to ensure that no one is listening to him. If no one is listening to him, then no one can later blame him if what he is saying turns out to be untrue.

apologist

In every bureaucratic organization, there's one staff member whose sole job is to apologize for all the mistakes made by that organization. Also, *flak catcher, glad hand,* and *shit eater.*

at that point in time

All-around buzzphrase particularly handy when a vague denial of blame is required. "No one was responsible for the error you're citing *at that point in time*" is an effective non-denial denial (because it sounds good but means nothing). The phrase briefly disappeared after being overused during the Watergate fiasco, but has now crept back into general use.

bafflegab

Strictly in-house term for probu language. *Bafflegab* is an untypically frank acknowledgment that official jargon is designed to confuse rather than to enlighten.

(to) bald eagle it

If a bureaucrat is caught with his (neatly pressed) pants down, and there's no one in sight, he can still try *bald eagling it, i.e.,* appeal to his accuser's sense of patriotism.

broadening colleagues' participation

Phrase for diffusing responsibility—and thus possible blame—for an action (or an inaction) by sharing the decision with several other staff members. As in "I know I'm the office manager and you're the office boy, Smith, but I'm a firm believer in *broadening my colleagues' participation* in departmental activities. Just sign your name here."

bureaucratization The process of dividing and then re-dividing authority, and the reason why it can take several bureaucratic agencies to get one simple job accomplished. (One example of the extremes of *bureaucratization* is that a salmon swimming up the Columbia River to spawn will pass under the jurisdiction of no less than 12 federal bureaucratic departments.)

callable credits Political and/or private-sector individuals who are accessible to a probu and who—more to the point—also owe that probu a favor.

cee gees Abbreviated form of Cradle to Grave. "He's a real *cee gee*" means the person in question was born a bureaucrat and will die (through proper channels, of course) a bureaucrat.

centrist In politics, the middle road between two opposite views; in bureaucracy, no view whatsoever. All bureaucrats, Republican or Democrat or Anarchist, are *centrists*.

clearance mechanisms The various methods by which a proposal is (finally) cleared for implementation. There are two basic categories into which these mechanisms fall. The first is a DC (or "direct clearance"), in which a department receives a problem and makes a decision on it. From the probu's point of view, this is bad management. Vastly more preferred is the SC (or "sequential clearance"), in which a department makes a report on the problem and hands that report to a second department that makes its own report and hands that to a third department that . . . etc.

counterpoint   The art of layering additional staff, organizational units, and even procedures to a basic program, much in the same way that a composer adds melody after melody to one basic theme.

CRONT   Code word reminding an interviewer what to look for in the make-up of a prospective bureaucrat applying for a position with his department: C stands for the intensity with which the applicant wants a Career with the unit; R stands for his Reasons; O for potential Obedience to the rules; N for Need to conform; and T for his belief in Team play. No one lacking any of these essentials can find a place in the bureaucratic life.

delphitic   A *delphitic* strategy means not making a move until all potential results of that move are first explored; *i.e.*, the use of specialized consultants to predict the possible outcome of an action. The expression is derived from the mythical Greek oracle at Delphi, who, incidentally, usually proved to be indecipherable in her predictions.

demute   Shout; argue; raise one's voice in anger. ("Be careful, Jones. Don't force me to *demute* at you.")

deproblemization   A term characterizing that most cherished of all probus' beliefs: Delay dealing with a problem long enough, and the problem will disappear.

DIM   Acronym for Directive Management; *i.e.*, a management style in which all personnel poli-

cies (such as dress, hair length, language, etc.) are controlled by a governing body. *DIM* is the exact opposite of Democratic Management; it's also the standard way of running a bureaucracy.

double A'ing Double Assigning; that is, departmental form of counterpointing in which two staff members are assigned (often unknowingly) the same task. The official reason: "Two heads are better than one." The unofficial reason: "Two heads are better to take the blame than one."

dynamic inactivism Much input, little output; the art, peculiar to bureaucrats, of appearing to be intensely busy without actually accomplishing anything. The expression comes from a private management-training company that once gave a course, publicly·funded, for federal-level bureaucrats on how to best fill their time without making an actual decision.

echosultants Probu jargon for a consulting team deliberately hired to come up with the same information provided by a previous consulting team. *Echosultants* are usually employed when a watchdog group demands that the bureaucratic department come up with a second opinion to justify its actions.

Edifice Complex A good pun characterizing a retiring bureaucrat who, after long years of service, now wants a park or building named after him.

EVS Labeling a proposal or already taken action, *EVS* is a disguised way to inform those involved to kill the project as unobtrusively as possible.

EVS is a discreet abbreviation for the equally discreet euphemism "Extreme Vanishing Silhouette."

exercising options　　The canny probu *never* makes decisions; instead, he *exercises options.* This way, he can always blame those who provided him with the options in case of error.

feet to the fire　　Buzzphrase for political pressure, the one known antidote to bureaucratic malingering. "We have to make a decision fast. Two Senators are putting our *feet to the fire.*"

finesse　　The Machiavellian ploy of using just enough power to gain your ends without using so much power as to inspire a counterattack.

gardening　　Euphemism, with a punny twist, for "hedging"; in other words, evading the issue by throwing up a protective shrubbery of bafflegab. "The department's been getting too much flack from that consumer-activist group. Call them in for a conference, and we'll do a little *gardening.*"

GIS　　Acronym for—well—acronyms: the Government Initial System. Senator James Wright wrote a poem based on just how confusing and absurb the *GIS* can be. A sample verse:
　　"The O-E-P tries to get help quick
　　　To disaster-hit towns that are stricken and
　　　　sick
　　　But the O-E-P works through C of E, S-B-A,
　　　　H-E-W, and H-U-D,
　　　Its own F-C-O and the D-O-T
　　　And how all this gets done is a mystery to
　　　　me."

(to) hornrim it	The cerebral bureaucrat's version of "gardening"; that is, hedging via pseudointellectual language.
illuminati	The small but powerful group of probus at the very top of the hierarchy. They used to be called the *elite* but that word's fallen into disfavor lately. *Illuminati,* however, with its double-edged connotations of religion and enlightenment, seems a dubious replacement.
in-basket situation	This expression refers to any problem or proposed action deemed too unimportant to remove from the drawer of a probu's desk. In the world of bureaucracy, most work can safely be labeled *in-basket situations.*
kainotophobia	An expression coined by social scientists (after a year-long study of the bureaucratic mind) to describe one of the two chief psychic disorders of the typical probu: fear of change.
kakorrhaphio-phobia	The second of those psychic disorders mentioned above: fear of failure.
klong	Intransitive verb used to describe the sinking feeling in one's gut when faced with a crisis of one's own making. The probu's major career goal is to avoid, at all costs, ever being *klonged.*
LOSS	Look-Out Situations. When *loss* is stamped on a report, it's a warning the problem contained therein is a tricky one that may, unless utmost caution is taken, explode in the probu's otherwise carefully protected face.
maximally valuable	Anything well-conceived by the bureaucracy is termed *maximally valuable;* any *maximally valu-*

able thing that turns out to be a minimally valuable mistake is *defundable*.

meaningful minimae

When an investigation produces nothing of value, the results are said to be *meaningful minimae*. (A literal translation of this phrase would be *significant insignificance*.)

morkrumbo

Nonsense phrase created by journalist Wallace Carroll to describe the probu's habit of awarding himself high-sounding but basically low-founded titles. Thus, on official reports, the office exterminator is *morkrumboed* to "animal welfare officer"; the secretary becomes an "administrative aide"; and the office boy wakes up one morning to find himself a "supply, systems, and transit engineer."

mumjummer

A bureaucrat specializing in bafflegab is admiringly called a *mumjummer*. Although there are several pun plays here—at first glance, "mumble," "mumbo jumbo," and "mum" (as in "mum's the word")—the meaning is clear; that is to say, it's an accolade awarded to anyone who can keep his meaning from being clear.

obscurate

To *obscurate* a report is to rewrite it to a point of total non-comprehension; the literary bureaucrat's version of bafflegab.

optimize

The conventional definition of the word is to make as perfect as possible. Perfection, however, isn't one of the bureaucracy's main concerns (if, indeed, it's a concern at all); when a probu announces, "I'd like to *optimize* sum factors before I opt for personal intent," he's really saying that he doesn't want to give an opinion until he's certain that opinion will cause him no grief.

orbital dialoguing

Committee talk; that is, sending a topic back and forth around the room until no one person can be identified with any particular suggestion for dealing with it. *Orbital dialoguing* is employed to break the logjam caused in an agency when a decision must be made but no one wants to be responsible for making it.

orchestrated rhetorical integrity

Officialese for language designed to confuse, conceal, or evade, but that doesn't contain any actual lies.

organizational osculation

A situation in which two separate agencies benignly touch closely ("kiss") at several points in common. If the contact isn't friendly, each agency will accuse the other of *organizational assault.*

pondynamics

The advanced course to the prerequisite, "inactive dynamism"; in *pondynamics* the student learns to be proficient in all those signals of deep thought—the furrowing of the brow, the pondering look in the eyes, the deliberate stroking of the chin, etc.—excepting, of course, actual thought itself.

postles

Bureaucrats banished from office following a political takeover, then subsequently reinstated when the original party returns to power. *Postles* is a bastardized form of the Latin word *postliminy,* an ancient Roman law governing the treatment of citizens exiled from the state.

preclude	Just as probus hate to say yes, they also hate to say no. Rather, they state that a proposal has been temporarily *precluded*.
probuistic	A professional bureaucrat planner's professional bureaucratic planning. It should be noted that only a *successful* plan is called "an unfortunate but inevitable fallback undergone to achieve acceptable countereffect levels."
procedate	To consider a problem in a linear, *i.e.,* straight-forward, fashion. *Procedation* is largely foreign to the bureaucratic mind and so is used exclusively in admonishment.
profing	Maintaining the proper profile in the office. If you wish to be noticed by your superiors, you come to work early, stay late, and write lots of memos; this is called *high profing*. If you've got reason to run for cover—after making a large and unconcealable mistake, for instance—you keep your door locked, brown-bag your lunch, and stop answering phone calls; this is called *low profing*.
psybus	Bureaucrats notably gifted at psychological warfare in interdepartmental feuds. If, however, their talents are officially recognized and employed to further their agency's—rather than their own—goals, they are then re-dubbed *psyops*.
residuate	An essential code word, *residuate* describes the bureaucrat's efforts to achieve the lowest of all possible profiles. The expression differs from low profing because it represents the probu's most desperate last-resort effort to hang on to

his job. "Green is *residuating*" implies that Green is in immediate danger of losing his position.

resonate   To be professionally *simpatico* with a colleague; to work well together.

sensorship   In-house nomenclature for the department in an agency responsible for collating the results of polls and surveys.

shellistic   An adjective used to describe any strategy designed to conceal both the nature and the authorship of bureaucratic policy. The expression is derived from the old con man's "now you see it, now you don't" shellgame.

shrdlu   Originally, this was printers' slang for typesetting errors; now, among probus, it's used to characterize a serious but nonetheless amusing goof. *Shrdlu* can also be a rather affectionate way of referring to a staffer who habitually commits such goofs. Finally, it is often used as a mild replacement for profanity: "This *shrdlu* report is driving me crazy!"

significantly   A deceptive buzzword universally employed throughout Bureaucracy Land to disguise the fact that a $100,000 publicly funded survey has produced zip results. "I'm happy to report that our department's study has created *significantly* viable output" is bureaucratic lingo for "We screwed up."

signoff   The *signoff* is that most dreaded moment when all the buck-passing has been exhausted, all possible exit routes have been sealed, all one's colleagues have conveniently disappeared in the field, and all one can do is put one's signature on the document and accept the responsibility for its fate.

stochastic

Newspeak for an old process: getting the jobs done through a trial-and-error method.

tall in the straddle

Half-sardonic, half-admiring description of a colleague gifted at fence-sitting indefinitely without ever making a commitment.

tay pay

Specifically, the dutiful political-dinner donation; generally, any dues-paying deemed necessary to job security.

thrustlust

Thrust is probu lingo for an aggressive attack. The *thrustlust* bureaucrat, like the "bloodlust" buccaneer, is addicted to not only defeating his enemies but to pillaging them as well.

toga

Half-hearted acronym for a whole-hearted belief; To get along, go along. As in "If you want a future in my department, Jenkins, you'd better start wearing a *toga*."

twiddlism

A bureaucratic ploy to eat up time in meaningless activity (*c.f.,* thumb twiddling). Probu A sends a memo to Probu B for approval. Instead of approving it, Probu B sends a memo commenting on the memo back to A. Probu A then sends a memo on the memo on the memo to Probu B. Really adept players at *twiddlism* can thus keep themselves happily—and safely—occupied for several months.

up to speed

Up to date; fully informed; conversant with the very latest details. The opposite condition—*i.e.,* ignorance—is referred to as *out of pocket.*

US
Ultra-stable; that is, a staffer who can always be counted on to hold onto his equilibrium. THEM, incidentally, stands for "Tends to Have Erratic Methods." (As in "Stevens is one of US, but Homer is definitely one of THEM.")

watchwaits
Probus whose fundamental and instinctive re-action to every crisis is to stand on the sidelines until the whole mess blows over. There's an understandable double standard implied here: if used as a self-description, it's a compli-ment; if used to describe someone else, espe-cially when it's you who must deal with the crisis, it's often an insult.

whipsaw
To take both sides of an argument simulta-neously. Not the easiest position to maintain, but essential for the efficient probu.

yesbuttism
An avoidance-of-responsibility technique in which a probu agrees to a proposal but makes reservations that can be placed on record—just in case.

zero-sum game
Playing for keeps; a conflict in which someone must win and someone must lose. The ongo-ing Bureaucrat vs. Public war can be consid-ered a *zero-sum game.* One guess who's winning.

The Power Brokers

Spook Talk

ac-op   Active Opposition; coded reference to enemy intelligence agencies. Also, *barbarians* (which is more accurate than insulting, as the word originally meant "aliens"); *indians; oons (i.e.,* "our opposite numbers"); and the *visiting team.*

agent   Anyone who, under the direction of an intelligence agency, is employed to gather information. *Agent* is actually a convenience word, too broad for precise definition. More specific forms include: *agent of influence,* an individual used to influence foreign nations' policy in favor of the United States; *confusion agent,* an individual specializing in misleading the enemy by false information; *double agents,* who work for one country by pretending to work for another; *in-place agents,* who—in the best spy-novel tradition—become citizens of foreign countries and wait, inactive, sometimes for years, before being used by their chiefs; *para-military agents,* trained to both encourage and aid foreign insurgency groups; *special agents,* who are civilians recruited either willingly or unwillingly because of particular personal skills; and *wad agents,* wad being an acronym for "waste disposal," waste disposal being a euphemism for murder—in more direct words, individuals who serve as hired assassins.

ammo   Alert Memorandum; a CIA document warning White House officials of any potential crisis brewing in a foreign country. As in "This alert's been dubbed *ammo* because of its unusually explosive contents."

artichoke   Capitalized, it was a U.S. Intelligence project—now phased out (supposedly, anyway)—

designed to ferret out traitors in the ranks by use of lie-detector tests, truth serum, and hypnosis; lower-cased, it's a generic term for any method of checking out one's own personnel. As in "Before the President goes abroad, his entire staff has to be *artichoked*."

aunt jemima
Euphemism for plastic explosives, first coined when it was noticed that they look like pancake mix.

backstopping
Providing the details of an agent's cover story to protect him from being detected as a spy. Typically, *backstopping* will include an entire—and entirely false—personal history, complete with fictitious parents, school records, etc.

BB's
Studiedly casual code word for cyanide death pills, usually hidden in a false hollow tooth, that are routinely handed out to agents before they begin a dangerous mission. Once bitten, these pills are instantaneously lethal, which is why these pills are called *BB's*: "Bite. 'Bye."

bib
An acronym for Basic Intelligence Background, which is all the information—social, cultural, geographic—about a foreign country used as a basis for U.S. Intelligence strategies and operations. As in "Time to put a *bib* on Angola."

bigot list
Misleading buzzphrase for the list of people allowed to have access to otherwise inaccessible information. *Bigot* is used here in the sense of "restricted."

blowback
Originally coined by military strategists to define a poison-gas attack that, thanks to an un-

expected shift of wind, drifts back over the ranks of the aggressor. As adapted by the intelligence community, *blowback* remains true to the spirit of this initial definition; that is, it describes any activity that backfires in the face of its planners. The rifling of Daniel Ellsberg's psychiatrist's office, for instance, was possibly the FBI's biggest *blowback* to date. Also sometimes known as *domestic replay,* or *fallout.*

BO   Acronym that officially stands for Biological Operation, and unofficially for Bug Out; either way it means the same thing: the use of toxic organic agents to kill or disable humans.

boos   The up-to-date files on the military strength of foreign nations. *Boo* is a reversed acronym for Orders of Operation of Battle.

botanicals   General term for all drugs derived from plant life that can be used as weapons against enemy forces. Some of the most recent *botanicals* can, supposedly, destroy military bases, destroy livestock (thus creating food shortages), impregnate private homes with noxious odors (thus creating household shortages), and cause human hair to fall out (thus creating, uhhh, hair shortages).

carnival   U.S. Intelligence buzzword for the not uncommon practice of creating and then monitoring a bordello for purposes of blackmailing and/or coercing rival agents. This, by the way, has brought a whole new dimension to the expression "undercover." *Carnival* is both a pun on "carnal," and a nondescript reference to fun and games.

collection	Any and all methods used to gather information. A *collection* may simply describe the buying of data; it may also describe murdering for data.
(the) Community	In-word for the entire worldwide intelligence-agency network, regardless of political affinity.
compromise	Documents viewed by persons, even persons on the correct side, not authorized to view them have been *compromised*. Documents rendered useless by such exposure have been *divorced*.
consumer	Either an individual or an agency authorized to use intelligence-collected information. In other words, the client. Also known as the *customer*, or *user*.
co-opts	Civilians who have been persuaded, either by friendly or by not-so-friendly means, to work for an intelligence agency. Up until recently, for instance, the CIA approached many American tourists planning to visit Russia and tried to persuade them to work as *co-opts*.
cop	Cover Protection; that is, the story used by a spy to conceal his real activities. As in "Commander Bond, your *cop* in Jamaica will be a sex-crazed life-insurance salesman."
country team	Buzzphrase for the senior members of U.S. diplomatic embassies stationed in foreign countries.
crants	Cover word for "cover grants," a fairly common U.S. Intelligence ploy in which private

groups receive public funds—the purpose always concealed beneath a fake project title—in order to do special work for the Agency. For example, one research company, secretly carrying out drug experiments on human subjects for the CIA, received a *crant* for an analysis "of the foreign-policy attitudes of Americans who own fallout shelters."

CRITIC Acronym for Critical Intelligence; that is, information considered so vital to national security that it bypasses the usual channels of communication and is directed immediately to either the President or a top official given dispensation to receive such material.

cutout Buzzword used to identify the person chosen to conceal all contact between members of a Black Bag team. For example, E. Howard Hunt's role in the Watergate break-in was that of a *cutout*.

deegee An abbreviation of Down Grade: the changing of a security classification from a higher to a lower level. Occasionally, *deegee* is also used as a euphemism for killing a turncoat colleague.

destabilize CIA-coined euphemism for the deliberate overthrow of a government—usually by financing insurgent native forces—that has been considered a threat to American interests. (The U.S.-engineered disposal of the Allende government in Chile is a prime example.)

disaffectors A foreign national, with valuable inside information, who defects to another country. Also, *disaffected personnel, emigré,* and *refugee.*

E & E

Coded warning, sent to endangered agents in the field, that it's time to make tracks for the border. *E & E* is the abbreviation for Escape & Evasion, an elaborate series of maneuvers designed to bring spies safely in from the cold.

eeto

Those measures designed by an intelligence agency to mislead a foreign power, usually by the manipulation of that enemy's intelligence system. The word *eeto* is made up of each second letter in the word "deception."

elicitation

An expression first used by the FBI—although now employed by most other agencies as well—to characterize an interview in which the person being interrogated does not know the purpose of the information being sought. *Elicitation* is a standard interrogation method when agents deal with civilians.

EMS

Electronic Measures; that is, the clandestine broadcasting of information via radio. Also, *ECMS,* Electronic Counter Measures, which is the jamming of broadcasts; and *ECCMS,* Electronic Counter Counter Measures, which is the jamming of jamming.

encrypt

The conversion of a plain-text message into an unintelligible (in the eyes of the enemy) form by means of various codes and systems. Spies being spies, there are also several other terms for the secret transmission of information. Among them: *cryptoanalysis,* or the breaking of enemy codes without prior knowledge of them; *cryptographic information,* or all classified documents and other written materials that describe an enemy's code system (when such information provides such potentially dangerous details as code keys or the location of transmitting stations, it's marked *significantly descriptive*); *cryptologic activities,* or all physical operations involved in the formulation, transmission, and decoding of secret messages; *cryptomaterial,* or all the electronic equipment needed for the code process; and *cryptosecurity,* or all elements involved in maintaining the system without its being detected by other intelligence agencies.

enduct Combined form of "end product"; that is, the final analysis of all intelligence material relevant to a particular project.

entity Buzzword for any private company, corporation, bank, or foundation that actively cooperates with an intelligence agency.

executive action Similar to *destabilize* in that it describes the overthrow of a foreign government, *executive action* is a CIA-originated euphemism for the assassination of the leader of that country. The term is still widely used, despite the fact that an American film that hypothesized that President Kennedy's murder could be traced back to the CIA was released under the title *Executive Action.*

expert Chilling acronym that stands for Excruciating Pain (this, by the way, is a buzzphrase for pain induced to the point of death) Employed by Rated Technicians (which is to say, specially trained torturers).

harsubs Combined form for Harassment Substances, which are various materials, more irritating than lethal, used against other intelligence agencies. Some of the more popular are stink bombs, itching powders, and diarrhea inducers. As there's little real value in the employment of *harsubs,* this reduces spies to practical jokers.

HIS Acronym identifying information gathered solely from a Human Intelligence Source.

human ecology At the time of this writing, *human ecology* is the official replacement for the older term "brainwashing."

I & W Indications and Warnings: intelligence activities intended to detect and report foreign developments that could prove threatening to the intelligence agency's parent country.

IDIOT Appropriated acronyn for International Developments Involving Overt Terrorism.

illegal Handy euphemism used to identify secret (and usually, though not always, unlawful) elements of an intelligence agency. Thus, *illegal agents* are operatives working in a foreign country without that country's knowledge or permission; *illegal communications* are secret messages transmitted without legal sanction from the nation where they originate; and *illegal residency* is an intelligence apparatus established in a foreign country without, again, official permission. Also, just as much in use is the suffix *covert.* (The opposite situation, *i.e.,* an intelligence agency working without any attempt at concealment, is identified as *legal* or *overt.*)

inners	Informants, usually highly placed officials in a foreign government, who work—sometimes for principle, sometimes for money, most times for both—with the CIA. Members of the reverse group, CIA officials secretly working for a foreign power, are called *outers*.
intelligence cycle	Intelligence is not information but is rather the patterns, conclusions, and actions taken as a result of that information. The *intelligence* cycle is the process—including planning, acquisition, processing, analysis, and dissemination—in which raw data are transformed into the intelligence enduct.
interception	The electronic plugging in to a rival agency's broadcasts is usually concealed under the heading *interception*.
joyces	Citizens of one country used by an enemy country for purposes of propaganda, usually via media broadcasts. The term can be traced back to one William Joyce, who, under his nickname Lord Haw-Haw, spread pro-Nazi information during World War II from a Berlin radio station.
lowblow	When an illegal agent is exposed, it's said that his cover has been blown; when his cover has been deliberately revealed—for one reason or another—by his own agency, it's said to be a *lowblow*.
minus advantage	The CIA first created this phrase to describe any operation—and they've had several—that left matters worse than they were before the operation was instituted. *Minus advantage* is synonymous with *blowback*.

motivation   Whatever convinces a foreign national to spy on his own government. Generally speaking, *motivation* is just a polite word for blackmail.

nasty   In-Community buzzword for "national security"; that is, the sometimes ephemeral excuse for denying interested outsiders—congressmen, reporters, etc.—access to information concerning any general U.S. Intelligence method or specific operation. As in "Don't worry about the press conference, Jenkins. Just play it *nasty.*"

nod out   Coded pun for "non-discernible microbinoculator," or any method of injecting a person with deadly poison in such a manner as to avoid detection during the subsequent autopsy.

noform   Nonclassified documents that are, nevertheless, marked "not for foreign dissemination."

notionals   Illegal agents will often claim employment by a fictitious private organization as a cover. An agent such as this is termed a *notional.*

penetration   An expression used solely to characterize the infiltration of a spy, sometimes called a *mole*, into a U.S. Intelligence agency. When we do it to them, it's referred to as a *double plus.*

pest   That is, Personnel Security; the means—usually consisting of rough background investigations—by which those people being considered for use by an agency are checked out for loyalty, patriotism, and trustworthiness. Sometimes called *pest control.*

phew   A rather strange acronym—considering that it represents the term "psychological warfare"—for the planned use of inflammatory propaganda to influence the actions of a hostile power.

phist   *Phist* (pronounced "fist") stands for Physical Security: all those measures—including alarms, guard systems, and barriers—that protect agencies against illegal entry.

plausible denial   A cover story enabling government officials to deny knowledge of an intelligence activity, even when they originally helped to plan it.

PM   Abbreviation for Pragmatic Methods; that is, any way of collecting information that succeeds. "Our agency works best in the *PM*" means the agency's guiding principle is that the ends always justify the means.

prit   Priority; the ranking of intelligence requirements by order of importance. Most agencies will periodically issue to their government controls a *prit list* that details the preferential ratings of proposed actions.

proprietaries   Private commercial entities actually established, funded, and controlled by an intelligence agency in order to sponsor clandestine activities.

raw   CIA buzzword for gathered data not yet processed into intelligence.

requirements   Euphemism for a White House request for certain intelligence information.

safe house	A literally innocent-looking house established by field agents so that they will be able to conduct covert operations in relative obscurity.
sanitation	Intelligence agents who specialize in disposing of the victims of assassination. Also, *waste disposal units.*
sanitize	The altering of a document, either by judicious editing or outright deletion, in order to protect the secret identity of sources and also the techniques of covert activities.
sensitive	Incriminating evidence that could, if revealed, wreak considerable havoc on the heads of an intelligence agency.
sheep dipping	The commandeering by an intelligence agency of either military equipment (like airplanes) or military men (called *sheep dips*). Also sometimes used to characterize the infiltration of a group (*e.g.,* a radical student organization) in order to establish acceptance in similar groups.
target of opportunity	Fortuitous accident in which information unexpectedly becomes accessible to an intelligence agency.
terminated with extreme prejudice	An agency assassination.

The Power Brokers

Law
and
Disorder
Talk

ACD In strictly legal terms, Adjournment in Contemplation of Dismissal; that is, although there is reason to believe a defendant is guilty, not enough evidence exists for conviction. The expression is also used, however, on both sides of the law, to describe a habitual— though not yet caught—criminal. "He's an *ACD*" means "he's one smart crook."

ace A one-year sentence. The word is often used as a verb, as in "I been *aced* by the court." Two consecutive one-year sentences are called *aces wild;* a three-year sentence is a *trey;* a five-year sentence is either a *pound* or a *nickel;* ten years is a *dime;* life is *max* and a lifer who has died in prison has *maxed out; ss* stands for Suspended Sentence; the generic term for any sentence is a *bit* or *porridge;* and a conviction requiring no jail time is a *walk.*

ack-acks Court-appointed lawyers. The expression is both a pun on the World War II antiaircraft gun and also a partial acronym for "ambulance chaser."

big time "He's *big time*" is a description of a prisoner who has both a long sentence and high status.

boxed Jailed following arrest, trial, and sentencing. Although there are literally dozens of expressions for being apprehended, *boxed* is the only slang word for being placed in a penitentiary.

cherry There's a divergence here between the law and the outlaw. For the police, a *cherry* is a suspect without any previous record; among criminals, a *cherry* is a gang member without any previous experience; to convicts, a *cherry* is a newly arrived young prisoner who has yet to be selected for sexual use.

crime in the suites
Lawyers' description of high-echelon white-collar felonies, as opposed to "crime in the streets."

flake
The deliberate planting of drugs or illegal weapons on a defendant's person in order to facilitate an arrest.

HAB
Courtroom jargon for Writ of Habeas Corpus. One of the last maneuvers by a defense counselor to free his client.

(a) jostle
An unsuccessful attempt to pick a pocket or snatch a purse.

OR
Initials standing for Own Recognizance; that is, released without bail and instructed to voluntarily return to the court for trial on a selected date.

paper felony
A form of plea-bargaining in which a defendant is allowed to plead guilty to a felony and so have that felony reduced to a misdemeanor. As in "The bad news, Rocky, is they got you on a felony. The good news is they're willing to paper it for a guilty-as-charged cop."

pee pee
The pre-pleading investigation by the Probation Department designed to ascertain whether the social environment of the defendant is conducive to rehabilitative training. The diminutive implications of the term, used exclusively by the Law, reflect the fact that most enforcement departments have neither

the money nor the manpower to devote much time to this form of police work.

pelicans   In-house nickname for appellate lawyers.

run a wire   Federal law enforcement code for setting up a tap on a suspect's phone or for planting a microphone in his apartment or office.

squash   That is, *quash;* that is, make a deal with the prosecuting attorney to get a charge dropped in return for a favor (usually information leading to the apprehension of a bigger fish in a bigger pond). As in "Listen, Counselor, I know who pulled the job. Wanna play *squash* with me?"

superseder   Legal term for one indictment that is so serious that it supersedes all other indictments on the same case.

2
Messages from the Media

Messages from the Media

Ad Talk
News Talk
Show Biz Talk

To whatever extent they avoid one another, members of the three media professions, News, Advertising, and Show Biz, share a particular schizophrenia: each is involved both in art as such, and in the art of turning a profit. In other words, a story, advertisement, or movie must not only *play* well but *pay* well, too. This commercial aspect irks all three, and the way in which they perceive their split roles and their split selves can be discerned from much of their jargon.

News people, whether in print or in television, tend to face up to the situation and shrug at the fact that the facts of life are what they are. On a small-town newspaper, for example, a general assignment reporter sent to cover a boring local event is known as *garbage*. A local television-news director, aware that covering only straight news might break the attention span of the viewers and send them to another channel, will order the anchor crew to *"HINT* it up a bit." (*"HINT"* is an acronym for "Happy Idiot News Talk," whereby the anchor men and women chit-chat and giggle—and in so doing, statistics show, build up the biggest ratings.)

People in advertising treat their art-versus-money schizophrenia with such total cynicism that Ad Talk includes not only a word for their chosen profession, *euphemantics* (an amalgam of euphemism and semantics) but also for the jargon itself, *zipvoc* (for "zippy vocabulary"). Also at the receiving end of this cynicism are: the media where the ads appear (television is *cluttervision*); and both prospective buyers (*concretes*, for "consumer cretins") and viewers who never buy a darn thing, no matter how persuasive the ad, (*lot lice*). Advertising, moreover, is a profession where demographics and consumer-testing play a dominant part and, accordingly, an aura of scientific knowledgeability also permeates much Ad Talk. For example, and at the simplest level, there is *DIB's* which stands for "Discretionary Income Budgets,"—or how much will they spend?

The amount of the take is also of perpetual concern to show-biz folk, to whom monetary failure—*i.e.*, no audience— has the additional ignominy of personal affront. (A newspaper that is never read or an advertisement that never sells surely can never cause such instant agony as emoting Hamlet's soliloquy to an empty theatre.) As a result, Show Biz Talk (extending the honored maxim, "The show must go on.") tends to put a brave face on things. If a play goes from beginning to end without benefit of an audience, the blame is not put on the performers but the competition, as in "there must be a *big dance in Newark*." If the apologist feels this is unfair to Newark, he blames the actual town where the disaster occurred, calling the place a *bloomer*. This stems from a double-edged insult used in carnivals: "The roses here must be blooming, 'cause this burg stinks."

Such real-life, tradition-based sources of jargon, good as well as bad, abound in Show Biz Talk. The *busker*, who performs on the sidewalk outside theatres for the benefit of those standing in line for tickets had the same job description and the same stage in Elizabethan England. The face of Annie Oakley, the star attraction in Buffalo Bill's 19th-century "Wild West and Congress of Cowboys Extravaganza," appeared on many of the free tickets he gave away; today, an *annie oakley* still means a free ticket. Turn-of-the-century vaudevillians often used a park bench as a base from which to deliver their corny acts; today, to *bench* still means to deliver corn.

Such jargon is also used by those involved in the more recent forms of entertainment—television and rock music. But their vocabulary of jargon is swelled by words that take into account the changing technical capabilities and moral values. Recording studio headphones to a rock singer, are *cues*; admirers of TV actors who send nude photographs are aptly called *fannies*.

Messages from the Media

Ad
Talk

acculturation   The period of time in which a new advertising campaign becomes implanted into popular culture. The most successful *acculturation* occurs when the specific client ad—"Pepsi-Cola hits the spot," for instance, or "Winston tastes good"—is transformed, at least temporarily, into a general public catchphrase.

aid   Stands for Area of Dominant Influence; that is, a regional area where a specific television station has the lion's share of the audience.

astronaut   A member of an ad team who is creative but nearly certifiably irrational. Every agency boasts at least one such "crazy," whose out-of-this-world behavior is tolerated because of his ability to come up with great ideas.

bambis   One of the more popular means to market a product is through the use of adorable, big-eyed animals; such ads are called, within the industry, *bambis* (after W. Disney's tremulous fawn). Perhaps the most famous *bambi* was Nine-Lives' Morris the Cat; his "autobiography" was on the bestselling booklists for almost all of 1977.

brainstorm   An agency meeting in which everyone is encouraged to throw out ideas, no matter how farfetched, in a sort of group-think free-for-all. The second meeting, held the next day, in which all the previous ideas are dissected, is called *braindrain.* Both terms are used, indiscriminately, in verb and noun forms.

cake mix   A curious situation in which the advertised
syndrome   product is *too* good for success. A few years ago, an agency tried promoting a cake mix

that required only the addition of water. After the product was tested, the agency discovered that housewives disliked it because they didn't have anything to do in the actual making of the cake. The admen suggested the company redesign its mix so as to make more work for consumers. The company agreed, and the product became instantly accepted.

clutter Jargon for all the various advertising spots on television. (There are three basic types of spots: *fixed,* that is, broadcast at a fixed time; *preemptible,* that is, broadcast at a certain time unless bumped by a sponsor willing to pay more for the slot; and *floating,* that is, broadcast at a time determined by the station.) *Clutter* is strictly a trade name used by insiders; to the rest of the world, the agency *always* refers to their spots as "commercials."

cluttervision The advertising world's general opinion regarding television and its place in society.

cognitive dissonance Phrase for the consumer's delayed reaction to being manipulated by a high-powered campaign into buying something he didn't really want (and now wants to return).

Com Com *Com Com* stands for a "Complete Communications" advertising agency offering a complete package that includes not only marketing but also public relations and survey services.

concepting Many of the more modern agencies offer clients a service with which their product can be pre-tested. A panel is selected from a list of "average" consumers, wired up to various machines (that gauge heart rate, perspiration rate, and so on), and then is presented with the product in question. In less technologically oriented agencies, *concepting* is used as a verb to characterize the thought processes in marketing. As in "I've given Smith the X account, and asked him to do some *concepting* on the palatability of chocolate-coated toothpaste."

concrete Hush-hush code word for the typical marketing audience. *Con* is an abbreviation for "consumer"; *crete* is an abbreviation for "cretin." To add insult to insult, advertisers separate concretes into various categories: *elite concretes* for upper-class buyers; *neat concretes* for the middle class; *sweet concretes* for women aged 17-35 (the single most powerful purchasing group in this country); and *beat concretes* for the largest income bracket—those transient Americans too mobile to be traced by creditors, and people who are simply habitual deadbeats.

cooper up Taking all the various ideas and themes and pulling them all together into one coherent whole. The expression derives from the cooper, a craftsman specializing in constructing barrels and kegs.

cosmetize Pretending to change an ad campaign, but actually trying to fool a client into thinking it's a new approach when it's only the same idea dressed up in new terms. Also, *painting the bus*.

CROC Committee for the Recognition of Obnoxious Commercials, created by one Bill Benson to provide awards (in the shape of toilet bowls) for those hard-working advertisers who, year after weary year, produce the most mind-boggling garbage imaginable.

cume	An abbreviation for the cumulative audience that an ad campaign snares.
dazzlefoot	An adman employed by his agency to dazzle a client with fancy linguistics and contagious enthusiasm in order to cover up the fact that the proposed marketing strategy is less than ideal.
DDT	Acronym for Derived Demand Trend, a characteristic typical of marketing in which the demand for one product creates the need for others.
demarket	A relatively infrequent ad approach instituted to actively discourage certain elements of the population from buying the product. The most successful *demarket* strategy in memory was the famous "Man's Country" slant for Marlboro cigarettes, which deliberately tried to dissuade women from buying the product.
destination advertising	Any marketing campaign that sells a product by identifying it with a certain type of consumer. Also, *direct connect ads*.
DIB's	Discretionary Income Budgets; that is, the portion of a consumer's income which can either be spent or saved. A *DIB's* ad is usually an in-store device created to inspire the consumer to buy the product on impulse (rather than as a planned item).
(the) drip-dry doldrums	A condition well known to even the most gifted copywriters and graphic artists in which they suddenly draw a blank on ideas. So-named because its victims tend to spend aimless hours at their desks, dry of creativity and dripping with sweat.

drive juice   The early-morning and late-afternoon hours when radio has its largest audience—primarily made up of commuters—and thus offers its juiciest time for agencies to run their spots.

eliting   Using high-gloss ads, the type that feature expensive-looking surroundings inhabited by expensive-looking people, that automatically slant the client's products toward the upper-class market (and upper-class prices). *Eliting* goods is a particularly effective strategy because it has a built-in safety factor; if the product fails to catch on with the high-priced spread, its cost can be lowered and it can be retargeted to a less exclusive consumer group.

ephemeralization   The built-in factor of any ad campaign encouraging consumers to appreciate that the goods they purchase have only a limited term of use. In the past, planned obsolescence was a fact of marketing life kept secret from the buying public. Nowadays, however, thanks to luminaries like R. Buckminster Fuller (who's been credited with coining the term *ephemeralization*), short-life products are viewed as essential to environmental control, and thus worth bragging about.

ethnicitizing   The exact opposite of *eliting;* that is, targeting a product to lower-class consumers.

euphemantics   Euphemisms + semantics = the advertising business. *Euphemantics* is an adman's word for his profession.

fash rash   An important part of any marketing campaign is to provide its audience with commercials that present attitudes, talk, implied relationships, and codes of dress currently in fashion. (Otherwise, the spots will appear to be out of date.) Fashions, like rashes, have a habit of coming and going very quickly.

flightpath A broadcast advertising technique that concentrates impact by controlling the number of times spots are aired over a period of time. A *horizontal flightpath* is an ad broadcast each day at the same time (which exposes it to the same audience over and over again); a *vertical flightpath* is an ad broadcast at various times each day (which exposes it to different kinds of audiences).

fluxum Word dating back at least a hundred years used as a generic term for any patent medicine. So-named because, in the old days, such products were guaranteed to cure anything, "including the flux."

Frankenslants Nothing inspires the truly creative adman more than being asked to promote a product that has absolutely no value to anyone. What's required, of course, is to establish a need for the stuff. *Frankenslants* are monstrous problems (like yellowing kitchen tiles), and horrific crises ("Oh my God, the bridge club is coming and my glassware is *spotted*.")

freebie feelies A ploy on the part of advertisers that persuades agencies to provide sample campaigns without getting paid for them. Often, after persuading several agencies to compete for their services, the client company will take the best proposal and initiate its own strategy.

fringing	Broadcasting ads just before and/or after prime time (7:30 P.M.–11:00 P.M.). *Fringing* spots is essentially an economic way of reaching audiences.
glad handouts	Public-service advertising used to build goodwill for the product rather than to inspire immediate purchase of it. The expression is a pun on *glad hand,* an old slang term for someone who sells himself by a strong handshake, a likable demeanor, and a smile stretching from here to there.
grinder	A spot actor, dressed in a white coat, who looks into the camera and solemnly intones, "Nine out of ten doctors drink Schlitz." The word was first used to describe the quack doctors who toured with medicine shows and now describes an actor posing as a member of any profession.
HAG	Acronym for Hidden Gay Appeal. Advertisers are faced with an interesting problem when dealing with the gay population. On one hand, the gay population represents a considerable consumer market; on the other hand, any overtly designed campaign might offend some straight consumers. The solution? Provide ads that seem heterosexual, but that also contain key code words and images familiar to the homosexual community.
HR	Heavy Roller; buzzword for the ad agency's client. This is a minor modification of the older term, *Big Wheel.*
hip-pocket	Nomenclature for an advertising man who can jump from one job to the next, all the

while upping his salary, because he has several lucrative clients in his *hip-pocket* that he can take with him from agency to agency.

hymns   Not only does the typical media ad provide various sneaky-Pete ways of pushing its product but it also contains concealed social messages—a mother lecturing a *dutiful* child, a married couple having a *friendly* argument— that reflect the type of idealized world in which the product would most flourish. *Hymns* is an acronym for Hidden Messages.

IMF   Acronym for Irritation Maximizing Factor. There are some media spots that try to sell their products through charm, wit, and even occasionally beauty; then there are others that push their goods through repetition and noise. This is *IMF*, the quality that makes a commercial so irritating it implants itself in our minds.

impact   If there were one buzzword to represent the advertising world, that word would have to be *impact*. Strictly speaking, it's the positive result of an ad campaign.

in the loop   Total involvement; working to full capacity on a specific project. As in "Gee, Smith, I'd love to help with the Nipsy Noodles campaign but I'm *in the loop* with the Tipsy Toodles account."

kickapoo   Any client's product, whether it be a Cadillac or a potato peeler, is referred to as the *kickapoo*. This is a frank acknowledgment of the advertising man's forefather: the medicine-show pitchman. Kickapoo was marketing's original success story, a harmless 19th-century herbal tonic that, through a judicious ad campaign, became a nationwide rage. Promising to cure "constipation, liver complaint, dyspepsia, loss of appetite, scrufla, impure blood, blotches on the face, scald head, and itching piles," Kickapoo Indian Sagwa, and its offspring, made its promoters almost instantaneously into wealthy people.

lemons
A notable, *i.e.,* lucrative, advertising campaign. Named in commemoration of the wildly successful, and epochal, Volkswagen magazine spots, the first of which admitted that even VW was capable of turning out an occasional "lemon" of a car.

lot lice
People who watch TV but who don't fall for the sponsors' pitches; from an old carny expression for local yokels who'd come to the midway early, stay late, and return home without spending a penny.

Merry Andrews
Agency lingo for spot actors who perform as the victims of headaches, eczema, acid indigestion, halitosis, rings around the collar, etc. In the 18th century, English quacks would peddle their patent medicines by planting in the audience confederates, called *Merry Andrews*, who—pretending to be sick—would sample the tonic, and then undergo immediate and miraculous "cures."

MC's
Money Coiners; that is, accounts so steadily remunerative that the agency representing them may as well be minting its own coins.

missionaries
Agency specialists who draw up preliminary promotion tactics for brand-new accounts.

nope comp	Acronym for Non-Price Competitions. Every once in a while, in order to goose sales, two similar products will declare war on each other through their ad campaigns (*cf.*, Avis vs. Hertz). If lowering costs is part of the battle tactics, which is rare, a *price war* has been declared; if the ads promise improving everything *but* the prices, it's called a *nope comp*.
nuisance parc	*Parc* is "crap" spelled backwards. *Nuisance parcs* are commercials designed to sell by irritating consumers to such an extent that the product name becomes implanted in their unconsciousness.
off-goal happening	An *off-goal happening* is an unplanned, but nevertheless helpful, by-product of a promotion campaign.
out to lunch	An ad strategy that appears rational enough but that, when more closely examined, is actually based on no logic whatsoever. A few years ago, an agency representing a soft drink company ran a series of successful spots suggesting consumers buy *two* six-packs of soda at a time so as to evenly distribute the weight. This was an *out to lunch* campaign.
piggy spots	Television and radio ads featuring someone in pain. *Piggy* is a code word for the motto "Pain Is Good," *i.e.*, presenting someone in acute physical discomfort is a good way to sell a pain-killer-type product.
playproof	"Let's *playproof* this campaign before we finalize it for presentation" means "Let's try to anticipate and correct every possible flaw in our

advertising proposal before we show it to the client."

PS

Public-interest ads done free of charge by the agency. *PS* stands for both "public-service" and—because they're incidental to the agency's interest—"post script."

psychographics

Mad. Ave. science for identifying the values and attitudes of the "typical" consumer. By using census statistics, demographics, and various tests and surveys, *psychographics* can supposedly suggest the most effective selling strategies.

quantifying

Advertising process devoted to dreaming up new words for the sizes of products, *e.g.,* "mammoth," "colossal," and "supercolossal" (for olives); "king," "queen," and "superking" (cigarettes); and the apparently endless "personal," "medium," "regular," "large," "large economy," "family," and "giant" (toothpaste).

(a) schnook in the nook

A low-level, highly irritating employee of the client who's been assigned to bird-dog the ad campaign for his boss and who proves to be more hindrance than aid.

segging

Short for "segmenting"; that is, targeting broadcast programming at a specific part of the viewing audience chosen because of age and income. *Segging* is a media strategy that allows the station to deliver a highly selective consumer group to the agency.

semantic differential

Conservative buzzphrase for an extremely heated argument. "We're having a *semantic dif-*

ferential with our client" can be translated as "The client's thinking of dismissing us."

serenity capability
Description of a talent for efficient organization. "Our Mr. Jones has a high *serenity capability*" simply means Jones will perform his job to the agency client's full satisfaction.

SIN Ratio
Signal Into Noise Ratio; *i.e.,* the amount of valid information as compared to the amount of useless junk coming out of a survey or research project.

sizzle sellers
Products that are successfully marketed because of their image instead of their contents; from the adage, "Sell the sizzle, not the steak."

slophop
Slop is an acronym for Smog, Litter, Overpopulation, and Pollution; the *slophop* is an ad campaign designed to improve the public image of a client—a car company, for example —accused of contributing to the mess.

softshoes
New breed of salesmen who depend on human psychology, not vocal power, to make points; the old-style peddlers, loud and pushy, are called *suede-shoes* because of their typically gaudier dress.

softly-softly catchy-monkey
An extremely low-key selling campaign, a tactic used by more and more ad agencies nowadays, derived from the mock-Chinese catchphrase used by one of the characters in Rudyard Kipling's *The Jungle Book.*

sour pipes
Angry letters complaining about shoddy products, written by consumers and addressed to manufacturers.

spaceheads Reference to the agency ideamen who are more concerned with high-soaring abstractions than with down-to-earth realities; the advertising profession's own version of the "absent-minded professor."

squirt it into the air (and see who it splashes) A suggestion that some idea or strategy be tested so as to gauge its effectiveness. This expression has officially replaced—in vocabulary if not in popularity—the bygone *"Let's run it up the flagpole and see who salutes it."*

subbing Implanting a subliminal message in a spot; that is, concealing a suggestion that appeals directly to the subconcious mind. Several commentators, notably Vance Packard, have long warned us of the various ways in which advertisers use "hidden persuaders," most usually sex, to sell goods.

tirekickers Industry name for pseudo-knowledgeable consumers, *e.g.,* people who pretend to know something about cars by kicking the tires (which usually only results in alerting the car dealer to their actual ignorance).

tooled-up Currently popular buzzphrase meaning intellectually well-equipped for the job, as in "Black's done his homework. He's really *tooled up* for this account."

turn the tip That element in an ad strategy or individual spot that draws in the audience. "They like the jokes and they like the glossy color, but it was that big-eyed child actor who *turned the tip." Tip* is medicine-show jargon for crowd; in the old days of the traveling shows, pitchmen would employ any method—parades, music, a staged fight, or a dancing bear—to draw the crowd's attention.

USP   Unique Selling Proposition, which is what the advertising game is finally all about. Each and every agency continually strives to create a *USP* for the client.

VD   Valley of Death. Some of the larger and more conservative agencies have what is known as Creative Review boards, that is, panels composed of retired agency executives who still wish to keep their hands in. These boards are considered at best a waste of time, and at worst a force interfering with creativity by the younger and more active employees.

velvet Overhead, salaries, and expenses eat up a lot of the agency's fees; what's left is *velvet*.

wise   Meaningless suffix tacked on to just about every other word in the advertising vocabulary.

Xers   Blatantly sexual spots; also sometimes known as *erector sets*.

zipvoc Generic term for the general lexicon of advertising jargon. Short for "zippy vocabulary."

ZOO agencies Contemptuous dismissal of the more rock-ribbed advertising agencies; "I work in a *zoo*" means "I'm stuck in a place that's Zero On Originality."

Messages from the Media

News
Talk

abjectives	Newspaper lingo, involving puns on abject, objection, and adjective for correction notices to previously published stories. (One example: "In an article dated February 4, Congressman Brown was quoted as referring to Congressman Smitt as a no-good, rotten, double-faced, two-timing, discourteous, and misinformed skunk. Congressman Brown has informed us that he never called Congressman Smitt 'misinformed.' We regret the error.") *Abject* because such notices are invariably apologies; *objection* because they're printed only in response to complaints from the injured parties; and *adjective* because they are meant to modify the original news report's effect. It should be noted, however, that as they are usually limited to two or three lines of small print hidden in the back section of the publication, *abjectives* rarely modify anything.
ACE's	Acronym for Accident-Coverage Experts; that is, those journalists specializing in the coverage of natural—and unnatural—disasters. The word is also often used in verb form, as in "Let's ACE the blaze" (meaning "let's assign the story on the fire to a reporter who's knowledgeable in the field").
A-copy	Technically, this describes the practice of publishing a public-relations release (or any advance materials) as "original" copy. Generally, it refers to any kind of lazy and/or shoddy journalism: "I'm killing your article, Burns. Reporting that the Police Commissioner's wife's a member of Alcoholics Anonymous is good. But implying, without proof, that she used to dance in a strip joint under the name of Bubbles is definitely *A-copy*."

advoes
Abbreviated form for practitioners of "advocacy journalism," a deliberately partial approach to reporting news in which the writer takes sides, makes value judgments, and sometimes even urges his readers to action. An updated replacement for the late 19th-century and early 20th-century term, *muckrakers.*

authoritative sources
Generic term for information given reporters by authorities who don't wish their names to be published. Even so, journalists have managed to create code words that, for those in the know, identify the origins of their stories. *Reliable source,* for instance, means someone in a position of power; *usually reliable source* means someone working for a powerful person; *sources close to the investigation* means either the police or the prosecution; *informed source* usually means another reporter; and *source of highest authority* always means the President of the United States.

backgrounder
Interview with a person who allows the reporter to use his story but not his name. *Deep backgrounder* is an interview in which neither name nor story can be published but can be used only for reference purposes (*cf.,* "Deep Throat," who blew the whistle on Watergate, but who was never directly quoted or identified).

balop
To pad out a print item or television story with graphs and charts; derived from Balopticon, an opaque projector used on TV shows to run illustrative materials. "This item's running short. Let's *balop* (pronounced "wallop") it with graphics."

boil

Editing a news story, bottom to top, is called *boiling* the article; cutting the story, top to bottom, is known as *baking* it.

boo(s)

Ghostwriters. Because of their writing skills—and because of their access to research files—many reporters do a little moonlighting on the side ghosting other people's books. Some of the most renowned journalists in the country have, at one time or another, earned money (but no credit) as *boos*.

bright

A brief, humorous, anecdotal news item. In newspapers, *brights* are usually printed at the bottom of the page to fill out an empty column; on television, they're more methodically positioned, often between two serious reports, to alleviate some of the gloom 'n' doom suffered habitually by TV-news viewers.

budget

Electronic-media buzzword for the compiled list of the day's major news events. It is from this list that the broadcasting director selects the stories to be televised.

chit editing

Sometimes, when handed a potentially inflammatory news story, the desk editor will take it upon himself to do some judicious trimming. In the upper echelons, this is known as *taking no chances;* among front-line reporters, it's called *chit editing*. Why? Because the word's composed of the first and last two letters of the term, *chickenshit*.

compo

Term for an article combining several real individuals into one fictional source who represents all of them.

crap

Straightforward acronym for *credibility gap,* the often staggering distance between what a political official says and what he really means.

crisis

Buzzword describing the fairly common journalistic practice of punching up a news story by finding some excuse to make it seem considerably more urgent and serious than it actually is. Always used as a verb, as in "We gotta find some way to *crisis* this piece on the local flower show. How about headlining it, GLADIOLAS FADING FAST."

culture vultures

In-house expression for the more sanguinary film, theatre, and music critics, who earn their living picking over the bones of a failed show.

curbstone interview

One of the more thankless jobs of journalism, involving long hours of standing outside some newsworthy individual's home in the hopes of collaring him for an impromptu question-and-answer session. Also sometimes called a *Pearl Harbor* (because of the importance of the surprise element).

double facers

Key words that qualify a news item. For example, "Senator Jones today indicated he might consider running for President." "Indicated," in this context, is so vague that it could mean anything (or, for that matter, nothing); other popular *double facers* are "possible," as in "Senator Jones might possibly run for President"; "believe," as in "Senator Jones is believed to be considering the Presidency"; and "alleged," as in "Senator Jones is alleged to be planning a Presidential campaign." This is known as no-news news reporting.

ears
A newspaper's *ears* are not, as you may have guessed, its reporters, but rather the boxes on either side of the nameplate on page 1. One contains the name of the edition; the other contains the weather.

embargaining
Special conditions imposed by a news source under which a journalist is given exclusive information only with the understanding that he will not release it until the source gives him the go-ahead.

ENG
General umbrella word for Electronic News Gathering; this includes not only television but radio, wire services, and satellite broadcasting. Print journalists have their own contemptuously dismissive expression for all such services: *HORE* (pronounced "whore")—Headlines-Only Reporting.

eunanchs
Another derisive term imposed on TV newscasters by print journalists, *eunanchs* are the carefully groomed anchor people who read the news items into the camera. The implied eunuch in the word is particularly pointed, as television reporters are extremely limited in terms of what they can and cannot choose to report upon.

falsies
A publicly condemned, privately encouraged journalistic strategy in which the reporter falsely identifies himself (as a police officer, say, or a friend of the family) in order to get information.

folo
Abbreviation for following up an original story with more detailed additional stories, as

	in "Hecht, I want you to *folo* that 'Man Bites Dog' piece."
fuzzbiz	Not very respectful slang for the police blotter, the law enforcement's daily record of crimes and the more serious kinds of misdemeanor.
garbage	Acronym for General Assignment Reporter, usually a beginner in the field who is assigned to all kinds of minor—and dull—reporting jobs, such as making market reports, preparing obituaries, covering local social events; in short, the litter surrounding major reporting.
gatekeeper	In-house name for the wire editor, responsible for monitoring the teletype machines. Called the *gatekeeper* because he's the one who decides what national and world news the readers will receive.
Gonzo journalism	Term invented by Hunter Thompson, a.k.a. Dr. Raoul Duke, to characterize the type of reporting in which facts are not as important as style, in which facts are not as important as gaudier speculation, and in which facts (in fact) are not important at all.
hint	Industry buzzword representing the phrase "happy idiot news talk." Practically all TV newspeople are now required to spend at least a few minutes of each broadcast in jolly, warm-hearted, and totally mindless conversations with each other. "Let's *hint* it a bit heavier tomorrow night" means the station director wants more news chatter on his show.

heart transplants	Gossip-column lingo for items concerning the celebrity sexual soap opera; *heart transplants* are the continuing record of who's dumping who for whom.
hellbox	Any article considered too hot to print and too good to discard is filed in a repository known as the *hellbox* until a final decision on its fate can be made.
high	Buzzword containing a partial acronym for the phrase Human Interest. Can be used in one of two ways: "We need more *highs* for the next edition" means the newspaper as a whole is short on human-interest articles (*i.e.,* brief anecdotal stories that appeal to the emotions); "Let's put more *high* in this piece" means that a specific story needs more emphasis on the human-interest element. Also known, though less and less these days, as *sob stories.*
keeper	A news story held back for publication until such time as it will have the strongest effect on public opinion. During an election, for instance, it's not uncommon for an editor to sit upon several *keepers* at once, waiting for the moment when they will do the most damage or good for the various candidates.
leaks in the ceiling	Information secretly given reporters from the top levels of power; information given from the middle echelon is called *leaks in the kitchen*; information from the rank and file is called *leaks in the basement.*
leave of abstinence	Reference to the governmental habit of tightening the expense-account belt each time a

new investigation or a new administrative organization is installed. (The implication here is that such Spartan abstinence will be all too brief.)

limbo   General term for graphics used on a televised news show, as in "Let's *limbo* the strike settlement." Also, *easel shots.*

mag   Abbreviation for "magnitude"; that is, the scope of a particular article in terms of potential readership. "What's our story's *mag* level?" means "How many people will be interested in the news item?"

ME(s)   Media Event; that is, an unimportant happening blown all out of proportion by massive press coverage.

MEGO   Acronym for "My Eyes Glaze Over"; newspaper parlance for an official government press release that will be used because of its importance but that is also unrelievedly boring. As in "The President's last statement on the energy crisis is a real *MEGO.*"

muggshots   *MUGG* stands for Marries, Unusual, Gorgeous, or Gone; *muggshots* are the in-house photos of various celebrities filed for use in case of marriage, an unusual occurrence, the paper's sudden need for a little cheesecake, or the person's death.

muster   A news story so important that reporting it is worth sacrificing other stories. ("I don't care if the front page is already packed up. Kill three columns. I'm making this piece a *muster.*")

NAG News Analysis Guru. Major newspapers typically have at least one person on staff whose sole job is to analyze the working reporter's articles for any important elements that might have been overlooked or misinterpreted. It's a high-paying, high-powered position, but most front-line journalists have —as suggested by the double acronym—ambivalent feelings toward the people who hold it.

newspeppers Those people, both private citizens and public officials, who are always good for a couple of quotes or gossip items that can "pep up" an otherwise dull edition. On a particularly newsless day, the city editor will assign his garbage team to go through the *newspepper* file and come up with a couple of paragraphs of titillation on one of the hotter subjects.

nudgement The skill to judge whether or not a potential news item is worthy of publication.

PISS Person-In-the-Street Stories, *i.e.,* interviews conducted with (usually uninformed) private citizens.

plant Counterjournalism ploy, usually on the part of politicians, in which one favored reporter is given an exclusive story that mainly benefits his information source. A reporter who's been so used one too many times is often referred to as *living in a hothouse;* a politician particularly skilled at the practice is said to have a *green thumb.*

play "How do we *play* the school scandal piece?" questions how the article should be positioned, headed, etc.

politigable   Media buzzword for unimportant press conferences called by an official strictly for purposes of self-aggrandizement.

pollution   Expression describing the proliferation of polls, censuses, and surveys typical—even peculiar—to this country. Reporters, who trust private opinion to about the same extent they do public policy, consider such devices the very antithesis of journalism.

prom   A news story that deliberately features a person or institution that's important to the community in which the newspaper is circulated (this will usually help sell copies). The angle on an identifiable public person or organization is called a *senior prom;* the angle on a private person or firm is a *junior prom.*

repeeps   Rewrite People; newspaper staffers who specialize in rewriting the story from the original reporter's notes. Really skilled *repeeps* can create a five-page feature article from a five-minute phone conversation with the on-the-scene reporter.

roorback   A slanderous, or at least outrageous, smear inadvertently printed as truth by a newspaper (usually because of political manipulation). This odd phrase can be traced back to "Baron Roorback," pen name of a writer who falsely claimed, in 1844, that Presidential candidate James F. Polk owned slaves.

RS   Acronym for Running Story, a hot news item that is featured for several days. Watergate, lasting as it did some eighteen months, was one of the biggest *RS*'s in journalism history.

rule-outs	Non-news stories published or televised on slow days when journalists are desperate to fill up space. So named because one of the sure-fire signals of such a story is the phrase, "The (name of official) absolutely *ruled out* today any chance of (whatever it was the official never intended to do in the first place)."

sacs	Code word for Sacred Cows; *i.e.,* persons or institutions held in such high regard in their community that they're generally immune from press attacks. There's a certain ambiguity here; *sacs* scrawled across a projected news story can, depending on the publisher, either mean "we have to kill this piece because it's too critical" or "this article isn't strong enough—let's really nail them."

segue	*Segueing* (pronounced "seg-way-ing") is broadcast slang for the transitional overlapping of dialogue, sound effects, or music. It's also general journalese describing the escalation of a particular news event: "That tax coverup is *segueing* from the municipal dog catcher to the state Governor."

severeheads	Television news commentators who specialize in analysis and interpretation rather than in straight reporting. An affectionate pun on Eric Sevareid, one of the grand old men of broadcasting. Also known as *pundits*.

shirttail	Technical name for late-breaking information tacked on the bottom of an already set-in-print news story.

specs	Abbreviation for "specialist reporters"; journalists who are expert in one field, such as economics, science, environment, etc.
spike	To hold a report for future use; to file a report for reference purposes. The term was derived from the old-timey editors' habit of placing such items on desk spikes.
snarlathon	Any and all political debates, which are (at least to the jaundiced eye of the journalist) more put-down contests than reasoned discussions of issues.
stringers	Part-time newspaper correspondents who are paid by the amount of space devoted to their stories. (Column length of the item is referred to as the *string*.)
sunbeams	In 1976, Congress passed the so-called "Sunshine Law" that opened federal records to the public and the press. *Sunbeams* aren't happy little pixies but rather are often grizzled investigative reporters who, taking advantage of the new law, are involved in full-scale reviews of various governmental files.
30	Time-honored journalists' sign-off to their articles, taken from the Morse Code symbol for "The End." (In the 19th century, on-the-scene reporters had to telegraph in their stories.)
thumbsuckers	Term for articles that are heavy on speculation and light on research. *Thumbsuckers* are would-be think pieces that haven't much real thought behind them.

ticktocks

Journalese for a feature article that provides the general background of a major news event; since such a feature is often written in chronological order—detailing day-by-day preliminaries leading up to the current situation—the term *ticktock* is an apt one.

tops

Abbreviation for "topics." In media jargon, *a tops day* is a day filled with lots of good news topics to choose from; a *topless day* is a day in which nothing very newsworthy is happening.

trendency

Journalese pun for news events more dependent on the moment's fashion than on timeless concern.

UP

Acronym for Upside-down Pyramid. *Pyramid* news refers to the conventional style of reporting, in which a story begins with the results and ends with the facts which led up to them. The *UP* is a particular writing technique, in which the most vital data are placed at the beginning (that is, the wide end of the pyramid) and the results are placed at the end (that is, the lower pointed top of the pyramid).

violin

In the past, the *violin* was an article written in unusually choice purple prose; nowadays, it's more often the lead—or cover—story in daily and weekly print media.

watchems

A general name for the section of a newspaper or TV news show dedicated to alerting consumers to various rip-offs and economic shortcuts. Also, *Hotline, Actionspot,* and *Soundoffs.*

weeds   Umbrella term for supposedly off-the-cuff re-
            marks made by a politician to reporters (al-
            though the statements were actually carefully
            prepared and rehearsed in advance). The
            journalists will usually go along with the ruse,
            in print anyway, and thus help create an un-
            earned image of wit and verbal dexterity for
            the official, but privately they are not fooled.
            The term itself is derived from the fact that
            many informal ceremonies presided over by
            the President, who is expected to have a
            phrase for every occasion, take place in the
            White House Rose Garden.

weirdos   Variations of squibs (small, inconsequential
            items), in which odd little news items are fea-
            tured (the most famous example of a weirdo is
            the headline: "Man Bites Dog").

WWWWWH   An equation every novice reporter must mem-
            orize that stands for the six basic questions to
            be answered in every news story: Who. What.
            Where. When. Why. How.

zooplane   Recently coined phrase to describe the dis-
            tinctly second-class transportation provided
            by political campaigners to TV cameramen
            and technicians (known among their journal-
            istic peers as *animals*). Any reporter who's in
            disfavor with the candidate he's covering may
            find himself riding in the *zooplane* (which, inci-
            dentally, can also be a *zoobus*, *zooboat*, or
            zoocar).

Show Biz Talk

acpo

Shortened version of *actor-proof;* that is, either a role or entire script so good as to withstand even the most inept actors' assaults. The phrase, however, need not only refer to actors but to anyone connected in any way with any of the arts.

angel

A backer of a show. It is probably not accidental that *angel* began being used by showfolk at the same time—the Roaring Twenties—that it was first being used by con men to describe the victims of their swindles.

annie oakley

Capitalized, it's the name of America's pistol-packing sweetheart. Lower-cased, it's a free pass for theatre admission. Even though revisionist history informs us that Buffalo Bill wasn't quite the great plainsman of song and legend, no one will debate his standing as a showman. During the thirty years of his "Wild West and Congress of Cowboys Extravaganza," he made it a constant point to hand out generous numbers of gratis tickets to friends, moneymen, and politicians. These tickets would often bear a likeness of Bill's sharpshooting star, and free passes to any type of entertainment have been called *annie oakleys* ever since.

B & O

Abbreviation for brass and overalls. Small circuses required their musicians (most of whom played brass instruments) to double as roustabouts (setting up the tents, the concession stands, etc.). Thus, a *B & O* show meant any circus troupe too poor or too cheap to hire straight laborers. Now the meaning's been expanded to include any company—be it the theatre, cinema, orchestra, or big top—in which the performers must also do the work of the stagehands.

bally

Originally, a free sample of what supposedly was being offered inside a carnival sideshow—most usually consisting of a few worse-for-wear carny ladies in bedraggled grass skirts executing a spiritless hootchy-cootchy. Even so, the free show was considerably more lively than what was waiting inside the tent. This is possibly why any prologue that promises more than its show can possibly deliver—a wonderful overture, say, to a horrendous musical—is now called a *bally*.

bench act

Initially, a vaudeville term for any particularly corny song-and-dance team. For some reason, such teams strutted their stuff on a set that would invariably include a park bench. The contemporary version of the phrase includes any tired old-fashioned routine, whether performed in public or in private: "I had a date with that producer last night. You wouldn't believe the lines he used trying to get me into the sack. Everything from 'my wife doesn't understand me' to 'you oughta be in pictures.' What a *bench act*!"

Big Bertha

The one, the only Ringling Brothers and Barnum & Bailey Circus. Named, so they say, after P.T.'s first big draw: Bertha the Rotund, "five hundred and fifty pounds of rosey-hued pulchritude."

big dance in Newark

The producer loves your show. The backers love your show. The critics love your show.

Even the stagehands love your show. So how come there's no one in the audience tonight? Must be a *big dance in Newark.*

bloomer

Any town where (show) business is bad. Most likely it's been derived from the old carny saying: "The roses here must be blooming, 'cause this burg stinks."

blue-shirt leads

Originally, a theatrical expression characterizing the main country bumpkin (a stock role) in the company. Adapted now by Hollywood to describe those leading men—notably Clint Eastwood and Charles Bronson—whose strongest appeal is with blue-collar income groups. The term can also be used as a modern replacement for "just folks," as in "On camera Joe may specialize in upper-crust roles, but off screen he's a regular *blue-shirt lead.*"

boffo

A solid success, regardless of whether it's an entire show or an individual performance. The roots of this word can be traced all the way back to 19th-century carny slang in which anything that was a good crowdpleaser—*i.e.,* brought in money—was called "good box-office." (This meant every and any event on the grounds, from Sally the Snake Woman to an impromptu fistfight.) Nowadays, showfolk use it to mark any successful endeavor, as in "Maybe it wasn't made in heaven, but while it lasted Liz and Dick's marriage was *boffo.*"

bofs

An acronym for Best Of (Albums); *i.e.,* a collection of hits gathered from a recording artist's various albums and reissued as a single record. As these releases are almost guaranteed moneymakers, the connection with *boffo* is no doubt deliberate.

bowdlerize

To censor; to sanitize a potentially suggestive performance or entertainment; to cut out, in other words, all the juicy parts. Generally credited to no less a personage than George Bernard Shaw, *bowdlerize* was created in honor of Sir Thomas Bowdler. A toothless and rather comic villain in the eyes of producers, actors, and the Floradora Girls, he was a 19th-century English editor who believed it his God-directed duty to expurgate all stage and literary works that passed through his hands. He was particularly irked by that well-known ponce and pornographer William Shakespeare, spending much of his righteous life attempting to censor all of the Bard Bowdler believed bawdy.

breathers

Films that have little going for them except *atmosphere,* which is itself a buzzword for the mood created by lighting, decor, and settings.

brodie

A turkey. Created in commemoration of one Steve Brodie, perhaps the greatest belly-flopper of all times, who, following a life singularly marked by failure, decided, in the summer of 1886, to end it all by jumping off the Brooklyn Bridge. In this, as in all his other career decisions, poor Brodie was doomed to fail. He survived his leap and lived another forty years, the butt of many a vaudeville joke.

Brodie's lack of success continued even beyond the grave. In the early 1960s, a musical based on his life and hard times opened on

Broadway. It closed three days later and, costing as it did some $900,000, is one of the most expensive *brodie's* in theatre history.

bullet
A record believed to be a potential success. The word's derived from the heavyweight trade magazines' (*Cashbox, Billboard,* etc.) practice of placing a large dot (*bullet* in the graphics world) in front of the names of those albums steadily rising on the charts.

busking the crowd
In Elizabethan times, the crowds queuing up for the latest Shakespeare or Jonson would be kept amused (and peaceful) by the *buskers*, street entertainers who performed songs, dances, and feats of magic. Long gone from the theatrical scene, *buskers* are now back in vogue—as many happy Broadway audiences waiting for tickets or taking an intermission break can attest. Not uncommonly, the show on the street often proves to be better—and less expensive—than the show inside.

catch flies
To attract audience attention; to upstage the other actors. In *commedia dell'arte,* the clowns would often mimic snatching flies from the air whenever there was some overly melodramatic turn in the plot. Today, the expression not only means any pantomimic stage action designed to draw attention away from the main business but also interfering with another person's moment in the limelight (*e.g.,* the cocktail-party star being upstaged by a waiter serving him his drink.).

chewing up the scenery
Overacting with a vengeance. Possible source is a 1930 theatre review by the acid-tongued

119

Dorothy Parker, who described one performer as "more glutton than artist. He chews up his lines, he chews up the plot, he chews up the other actors, and when nothing edible remains on stage, he commences to *chew up the scenery*."

china circuit

Originally, a notably tacky road tour that wound its doleful way through several Pennsylvania towns whose sole claim to fame was in the manufacture of china chamberpots. Now, any execrable circuit tour.

closing the door

An extremely effective exit line. "Leave my house," says the heavy, "and never darken the door again." "I will leave gladly," replies the heroine, "for to live under this roof one moment longer would be to bear forever the shame of your vile presence." That's a *boffo* line. Reenter the heroine. "And another thing," she cries. "God bless America!" That's *closing the door*.

cold house

The most typical industry reason for the failure of a play or film. ("That *house was so cold* even Laurence Olivier doing a striptease wouldn't warm it up.") There are several other popular expressions describing a less than successful event. *An opener and closer in one* is a strictly neutral way of characterizing a show doomed to an early demise. From then on, the terms become more and more explicit—ranging from the ever popular *laying an egg* (1929 *Variety* headline: "Wall Street Lays Egg") to the ultimate *El Stinko* (a phrase usually accompanied by painful grimaces, rolling eyeballs, and the firm holding of one's delicately averted nose).

Show Biz Talk

cues
Rock musicians' slang for headphones; called *cues* because they're worn in recording studios by musicians who otherwise couldn't hear the other band members.

cutes
TV industry pun for film cuts to the faces of actors who specialize in piquant expressions and gestures.

CW
Record-business code standing for Comfortably Weird; that is, someone who has achieved success in the industry without losing his individual eccentricities.

fannies
Television slang for particularly ardent fans, many of whom send candid (read: nude) photographs of themselves to their favorite TV celebrities.

favored nations clause
In the performing arts, the term's been adapted to describe a contractual clause that assures the star he's getting the very best deal in the project. Only the biggest—and most secure—performers can gain this kind of diplomatic recognition.

flopsweat
There you are. Center stage. In the limelight at last. Calm and confident, equipped with fifteen minutes of gen-u-wine, socko, rapid-fire comic patter. The only trouble is someone forgot to tell the audience to laugh. They're not laughing. They are not laughing. What they are doing is staring. And coughing. And muttering behind their hands. Jeez! Did someone just say something about a lynch mob? Every performer has experienced this at least once: a dead house, no place to go, and the *flopsweat* beginning to trickle down neck.

fly on the wall	Cinema lingo for the movie camera; so-termed because it objectively records events without playing a part in the action. Often shortened to *fly-on*.
foreground noise	Film and TV in-house slang for dialogue, indicating the relative unimportance of spoken words to most visual artists working in the fields.
four & three	Any theatrical company not located in New York City. *Four & three* used to be the name for the small repertory troupes who'd boast four men and three women in their permanent casts.
FTC promotion	Buzzword, universal to all branches of show business, for promoting an event despite bad reviews. FTC stands for Fuck The Critics.
geek or glom	A rather subtle distinction between two choices: one is out-and-out rotten, the other is merely bad. A *geek* was a sideshow performer who swallowed live mice, rats, chickens, and snakes. A *glom* was a sideshow performer who only *pretended* to swallow mice, rats, etc. Although it's a difference best to be appreciated by the *geeks* and *gloms* themselves, the phrase is widely used by more respectable—not to mention better fed—entertainers today.
give the skull	Television comedians' slang for a fast (facial) reaction to a line of comic dialogue or action. The opposite reaction is called a *slow take*.
grouch bag	Communal kitty kept by a road-company troupe just in case the producer disappears one late night with the box-office receipts.

(Most standard actors' contracts include a clause providing a separate salary to be included in the *grouch bag*.)

HIP   Acronym for High-Intent Priority. Any record album designated a *HIP* hit is slated for an all-out, twenty-gun-salute advertising buildup.

in one   An old theatre expression for "down center," the most prominent position on the stage. Nowadays, a performer (any performer in any medium) who's in the midst of a real audience-grabbing scene is said to be *in one.* The term is also often used to describe the private antics of an entertainer who insists on always being the center of all attention.

IN's   Acronym standing for Initial Nibbles; that is, the very first reports of how a film or record album is selling. The final reports are *outs.*

iris   In the very beginning days of movie-making, a favorite device was the *iris, i.e.,* a scene in which the camera lens slowly closed until only one actor—usually the star—was visible. Since the lens closed in a circular fashion, the actor was framed by what appeared to be a halo. Today, "Let's *iris* this scene" is both film and television jargon meaning "Let's make this scene as sentimental as possible."

leerics   Music-business code word for a rock sub-genre: suggestive (but never explicit) sexual lyrics (*cf.,* the hit, "Yummy, Yummy, Yummy, I Got Love In My Tummy").

Memory's Little Helper   Rock musicians' lingo for the recent addition to the recording studio: computers.

123

Monday worker	Backstage euphemism for a colleague who steals from the other actors (usually by riffling through clothes in the dressing room). From the classic children's book *Toby Tyler,* in which *Monday worker* was used to describe thieves who'd steal clothes from backyards while the townspeople were watching the circus parade.
MOR	Record-industry acronym for Middle of the Road; the term both describes a certain type of music (basically, very soft rock) and also indicates the kind of audience this music attracts ("middle" since the audience in question is predominantly middle-class, middle-aged, and middle-American).
mouth	"What's the *mouth* on the show?" means "What kind of reviews did we get?" Not to be confused with *worm,* which is show biz talk for "word of mouth."
nope	Acronym standing for No Promotion. If a record company doesn't think its latest album has a chance, the album's marked *nope* and sent to the remand bins.
nudge shows	Essentially harmless comedies that specialize in very lighthanded risqué material. They're called *nudge shows* because their audiences tend to elbow each other at every double entendre.
pals	Studio musicians who are used to augment a rock group's album. *Pals* is a shortened version of both "paladins" (medieval knights who roamed the countryside) and "Paladin" (the main character of the popular late-50s television show "Have Gun–Will Travel"). The em-

phasis is on the hired-gun nature of these usually anonymous but gifted minstrels.

Patch Always-capitalized nomenclature for any and all show-business lawyers.

phoner This is a slang word common to Broadway and Hollywood that describes any patently false plot device. There's a double pun at play here. The first, and most obvious, one is on "phoney." The second is based on a still-used stage convention in which one of the characters (often the maid) is "discovered" at the beginning of the second act speaking on the telephone. "No, I'm sorry," she might say. "Mother can't talk to you now because she's meeting her lover in a seedy hotel downtown. Father can't talk to you now because he's a secret alcoholic and is presently drinking himself insensible in the den. Sister can't talk to you because she's having her third post-puberty crisis this week, and Junior can't talk to you because he was arrested at the climax of Act One."

prewashers Music-business slang for those executives who are basically uptight and unhip but who nevertheless insist on dressing in such a way (prewashed denims, etc.) that would suggest the opposite. Also, the oxymoronic *washed funk*.

RAP That is, Radio Air Play. "Hey, our record's really being *RAPed* this week" is a way of announcing that the album's receiving a lot of deejay attention.

redlight Television expression for a stock turn of dramatic events that is designed to create a stock reaction among the audience (fear, joy, relief, etc.). It's been named a *redlight* because the audience response is as predictable as is a driver's response to a red traffic light.

(a) risley act

Arthur Risley was once a popular English music-hall star who earned his fame juggling the boards, but his name survives as a generic term describing any strange performing skill (*cf.,* playing musical spoons or conducting a pack of musical dogs). On the billboard of the production team for television's *The Tonight Show* is the following admonishment: "Remember. Johnny wants two *risley acts* a week."

schlock stock

Movie-industry rhyming phrase for an as yet unedited film. *Schlock* is Yiddish for "junk," but this fact has nothing to do with the quality of the movie itself.

shit

Musicians' term and an acronym of sorts for Hit Single.

slums

An actor who's just going through the motions of performing, without really exercising his craft, is said to be "working in the *slums.*" *Slums* is an old carny word for the cheap merchandise handed out as prizes by the test-your-skills booths on the carnival strip.

surp

Trick practiced by many stage actors. After a particularly enthusiastic series of curtain calls, a performer may deliberately pretend to be caught unawares when the curtain rises yet again. The *surp* (*i.e.,* "surprise bow") permits the actor to blush prettily, mime amazement and humble gratitude, and show the properly impressed audience that, under the make-up, he's just plain folks.

tasty

As of this writing, *tasty* is the record world's slang word for "great," and —as such—is the official replacement for *bitchen, boss, groovy, heavy, mellow,* and other equally dated accolades.

tenay deejays

Disc jockeys forced by program managers to play the same Top-Ten (actually, in most cases, it's the Top-Forty) records over and over again. As this is not a very stimulating livelihood—leading, as it often does, to boredom beyond belief or control—a *tenay deejay* is also slang for any atrocious job, in or out of the record business.

three-sheeting

Once *three-sheeting* described the small-circus practice of plastering a town with advertising posters; now it's a general buzzword for inordinate and unjustified bragging.

throwing babies

The highest praise one can pay a stand-up comic is to tell him after the performance that the audience "loved you so much they were *throwing their babies* from the balcony."

tithit

Music industry acronym for Turntable Hit; *i.e.,* a single that receives a lot of radio airplay but that doesn't sell very well in the stores.

tweenies

The brief passage of dialogue and plot exposition inserted between the sex scenes in porno films.

up

Theatrical jargon for missing a line or cue; also any general foul-up ("getting married was the biggest *up* of my life").

valentines

Generic term for the posters advertising various attractions on the carnival midway. Usually painted on canvas, often genuine if primitive works of American art, *valentines* usually promote such crowd-drawers as fat ladies, human skeletons, mostly naked mermaids, pinheads, Siamese twins, and Rollo the Dog-Faced Boy.

wipe   General show business term for being fired before completion of the show, probably derived from the now old-fashioned cinema device that dissolves from one scene to the next by a lens technique resembling a windshield wiper.

zzz   Private movie-industry joke identifying G-rated (that is, child-oriented films), which are typically wholesome, upstanding, and sleep-inducingly dull.

3
The Technocrats

The Technocrats

Computer Talk

Military Talk

The dubious honor of being the most popular target for public abuse can probably be shared equally by computers and the military. Behind the computers that "make the mistakes" of the telephone company and the weapons-systems experts who figure out the costs of defense, stands a host of technocrats—scientists, engineers, technologists, and technicians. They, too, have their jargon: Computer Talk for those who inhabit a world whose flora and fauna are made of stainless steel, and Military Talk for those who live in a well-nigh identical environment, but whose jargon is occasionally more apocalyptic.

As might be expected, Computer Talk abounds with jargon related to space travel, including such words and acronyms as *avionics* (the adapting of electronic systems to travel in space), BURP (the jarring motion caused when the on-board computer adjusts direction) and *cesspool* (a spacecraft system that converts waste to, among other things, food). The jargon of landlubbering computer experts includes *glitch* (an unexplained energy surge), *flopsy* (a flexible memory-storage disk) and *badger* (a computer terminal that can "read" identification badges).

Both extraterrestrial and terra-firma computer experts might seem at a glance to be entirely devoid of emotion. This, if their jargon is anything to go by, is not always the case. Many have a genuine liking for computers (a machine held in particular affection is a *kludge*); in fact, they apply certain elements of Computer Talk to computer and human behavior patterns alike. A *gang punch*, for example, means either the punching of identical information onto a number of cards or, what other professions know as a gang bang. *Freefall*, the condition of weightlessness in space and a consideration in designing spacecraft computers, also means "falling-down drunk." DO (decision overload) is the malaise of both a computer that is nonfunctional because it has been overly programmed and an executive who has collapsed from strain. (Such strain, incidentally, might stem from having made too many *beepers*, Computer Talk for human, rather than computer ideas and solutions to any given problem.)

In contrast to Computer Talk's occasional acceptance of the existence of human beings, Military Talk goes to great lengths to avoid all mention of flesh and blood. *Friendly casualties*, are our own wounded and dead. They are the result of fighting the enemy, or in other words, of having made *contact* with *hostile unfriendlies*. This reluctance to refer to human beings applies in particular to the jargon related to atomic, biological, and chemical warfare—an event which itself, through its interests of A, B, and C gives us the terrifying threat of *alphabet soup*. (The bacteriological scientists who work on plans for biological warfare—or, let's face it, germ warfare—are known as *bugs bunnies*.)

The very worst that could ever happen—an accidental nuclear war and the resultant worldwide destruction—are known in Military Talk by two all-too-apt acronyms: OOPS, for "occasionless ordered preemptive strike," and MAD for "mutually assured destruction." (The notorious button by which an American president can launch such an OOPS and create such a MAD is actually a set of codes carried by a military officer who never leaves the president's side. The officer is known as the *bagman*, the case, *the football*.)

Many of these Military Talk phrases are the product of public-relations men ("flacks" in every other jargon but the military's) whose skill in euphemisms knows no limit. Fortunately, for the rest of us, Military Talk is occasionally brought back to ground by the saltier jargon of the GI. Whereas a military flack might describe battle fatigue as *acute environmental reaction*, to the GI it is more simply, and more accurately, *lurped out* (from LURP, a long-range reconnaissance patrol, one of the most dangerous and *friendly-casualty*-pronc details of the Vietnam War).

And to whatever degree the rest of the world (*i.e.*, the nonmilitary population or, to Military flacks, the *nonessential personnel*) might be threatened by disaster, the GI can't wait to join us. *The Real World* has always been his objective, and to get here he has to get out of the service (a process he thinks of as *derosing*), even if it does mean a reentry into a life where telephone bills are always the victim of computer error.

The Technocrats

Computer Talk

aart
Industry code word for computer-produced artworks. Within the past two decades, artificial-intelligence machines have "created" their own stories, poems, essays, drawings, music, and animated films. Limited by its dependence on a purely numeric system of logic, *aart* is not, of course, art. Not yet, anyway.

aerodynamic personnel decelerator
NASA has invented so many imponderable buzzwords that it would be futile to list them all, but this is the first phrase in their private lexicon. *Aerodynamic personnel decelerator* is but a spacey way of saying *parachute*.

afterbody
Astronaut lingo for a companion body—which can be anything from a spent vehicle to an empty beer-can—that follows a spacecraft as it orbits. However, the word is also used by computer technicians in a more personal sense to describe a secret lover.

algy
Nickname for "algorithm"; that is, the mathematical (and philosophic, too) concept in which a problem's solution is sought via a set of ordered steps and/or calculations. This is the principle behind not only computer science itself but also the entire technocratic approach to life. Although the word is most often used as a noun, it can also be employed as a verb. "No need to panic. All we have to do is *algy* the problem, and we'll have the answer in no time."

anomaly
The NASA Mission Control people never say something is going wrong; instead, the crisis is always referred to as an *anomaly*. If it goes according to plan, it's *nominal*.

artificial intelligence	The generic name for any computer system. (There are, basically, two types: analogs, which measure physical properties—voltages and currents, for example—and which are mostly used to solve engineering problems; and digitals, which translate problems into numeric equations, and which are used for everything from controlling nuclear missiles to playing chess.)
assemble	Essential buzzword characterizing the overall process of gathering data, translating it into computer language, programming it, and interpreting the results. Also used by technocrats to describe a readjustment of personal habits, goals, needs, etc.
ATOLL	Technically, an acronym for Acceptance Test Or Launch Language, *i.e.,* the computer program used for checkout purposes just before launching a space vehicle. Again, however, it's been adapted for private use. The lower-cased version, *atoll,* refers to last-minute calculations prior to committing oneself to a new course of action.
avionics	Describes the science of adapting electronic systems (including computers) to spaceflight. Also, sometimes called *astrionics.*
badger	A computer terminal designed to read special badges identifying personnel. There's a pun in the expression: unless the terminal approves the ID, the entrance door remains closed (like a *badger* defending his nest).
bandwith	Futurologists' in-word for environmental conditions. "Man has to switch *bandwiths*" can be

translated as "Man has to change his environment."

BASIC   Acronym for Beginner's All-purpose Sym-
bolic Instruction Code, which is an easy-to-
learn computer language used to train
fledgling programmers. The word also is
employed to identify the novices themselves,
as in "Go easy on Joe. He's still *BASIC*." The
computerese version of *tenderfoot*.

beeper   Human, as opposed to electronic, ideas and
solutions. "The computer's dry on this one.
Let's try some *beepers,* instead." The word is a
combination of "brain" and "processes."

biofeedback   A recent application of computers in which
humans are taught how to consciously control
such body functions as heartbeat, blood pressure, and creative brain patterns.

bit   Technically, an acronym for "binary digit," the
smallest unit of notation in the basic computer
language. *Bit grinding* is slang for the processing of data info into a computer; *twiddler* is a
jocular way of characterizing the computer
programmer himself.

black box   Sinister expression for a piece of technical machinery that functions in a predictable fashion
but that contains inner workings that are a
mystery to the user. By extension, *black box* describes any inexplicable condition of human
life, as in "To tell you the truth, Buzz, sex has
always been a *black box* to me."

blue collar   Not a unionized computer but rather one that
is employed in factory work. Computers used

in offices are, naturally, called *white collars.*

breadboard
There are two dated meanings for this expression: 1) the board on which an electronic assembly is mounted; and 2) the initial assembly of all information needed to arrive at a conclusion, as in "Let's *breadboard* the problem before we try to solve it."

breakaway
Also called the *breakaway phenomenon,* it is the occasional feeling during spaceflight of being totally isolated from all other humans still landlocked back on earth. Astronauts and mission control computer scientists will often characterize a brief bout of depression as a *breakaway.*

Brenschluss
From the German; literally, "burn-end." Once employed to describe the cessation of a rocket's firing; now, as NASA is no longer quite so crowded with German scientists, used as jargon for exhaustion. "You keep working so hard, Neil, you'll end up *Brenschluss.*"

brute force
Mathematicians' term for a technique requiring the raw power of a computer. An elegant breed, mathematicians have been known to resent equations that don't reflect the end product of human reasoning; thus, the derisive implication of the phrase.

BURP
A less than genteel space-age acronym for Backup Rate of Pitch; *i.e.,* the slight jarring movement of a rocket ship as its onboard computer adjusts its position.

burst
To tear computer-printed output along its perforated edge and separate its sheets.

caveman

In-vernacular for an outdated, or malfunctioning, artificial intelligence system. As in "We have to persuade the boss to get us another machine. This computer is *caveman*."

cba

Lower-cased abbreviation for a computer-based automaton; that is, a piece of machinery (usually, though not always, part of an assembly line in a factory) that's hooked up to an artificial intelligence device so as to improve the speed and accuracy of production. A harmless appearing phrase, *cba* has proved to be the rallying cry for many a labor strike (unions having a well-grounded fear of machines replacing men).

cesspool

Space terminology representing an enclosed system that provides life support in an isolated chamber, particularly a spacecraft capsule, by means of a chemical cycle converting waste products into oxygen, water, and food. *Cesspool* is a semi-acronym for Closed Ecological Systems.

chad

Specifically, the piece of material removed when punching a hole in perforated computer tape; generally, any wasted—*i.e.*, unused—material, information, or ideas. As in "I keep coming up with these great concepts, and my boss keeps converting them into *chad*."

Chinese laundry ticket

A computer-language code in which symbols are arranged in columns reading from right to left, as with Chinese script.

cogless

To feel *cogless* is to feel that one is no longer part of the machinery of life.

configure   Another technological word released from the drawing board into personal use, *configure* is merely an elaborate way of saying "to follow." As in "Yeah, it's true. I hired a private detective to *configure* my wife."

construct   A working model—a spacecraft, for example—used in operational and/or computer research before building the real thing.

CRAM   Acronym for Card Random Access Method, particularly well-suited as it describes an auxiliary storage device that can cram great amounts of computer data (in magnetic form) into a very small space.

crosstalk   Literally, the aural effect occurring when unprogrammed energy jumps from one computer circuit to another circuit. Not so literally, unnecessary argument ("Don't give me any *crosstalk*, Smith. Just do your job!"). A good cross-reference is *static*.

cybers   Informal slang for scientists working in the field of cybernetics, the comparative study of mechanical and human communications systems.

datamation   Jokey generic term for dating services that match prospective mates through the use of computers.

debug   To locate and correct computer malfunctions; likewise, to correct any personal errors in one's life.

D O   Abbreviation for Decision Overload, a condition peculiar to high-pressured, in-charge technocrats forced to continually make top-level pronouncements on a wide variety of essential issues. "I'm afraid Bill has *D.O.'d*"—note, by the way, the pun on *"O.D.'d"*—means poor Bill has made one too many decisions and consequently is suffering now from an inability to make any moves at all.

doobies Acronym for Data Bases; that is, the collections of information forming the foundations of computer programs. Also, technocratic slang for life itself. A screwed-up computer program is called a *screwby doobie*.

dummies *Dummies* are false instructions deliberately inserted in a program to test the computer's ability to ignore illogical data when solving a problem.

econothink Futurologists' buzzword for any technological system that is motivated solely by the need for profits and that, in the process, ignores the human factors involved in social and economic change. Also *econocentrism*.

entropy In physics, which first coined the word, *entropy* describes the inevitable dissipation of energy and matter into inert waste. Among technologists, the word's come to characterize the amount of disorder in their particular system. Thus, *low entropy* means high organization; *high entropy* means low organization. Too much *entropy* in a system will lead to chaos.

error terrors Print-out admonishments. During their training period, novice programmers tend to make many mistakes. The teacher computers are typically set up to not only indicate each mistake but to also read various sarcastic elements—"Wrong again, you dope," for instance, or "Go stand in the corner, duncehead"—for its embarrassed students.

exbiology

To date, the most advanced of all computer-based sciences; namely, the hypothetical study of extraterrestrial life forms.

experieaks

Combined form of "experiential freaks." Futurologists maintain that we are rapidly developing into a race of beings desperate for constant sensory gratification. (There are also many social scientists who contend we've already reached this point.) To cite just one example: the gambling casino of tomorrow may offer experiential payoffs rather than merely money; a night with a beautiful star if you win, a day in solitary confinement if you lose, and so on.

exponential smoothies

Long-range forecasting techniques designed to smooth out any wrinkles in a project before the project is initiated.

eyeballs in, eyeballs out

Astronaut lingo used to characterize both the acceleration experience at takeoff (*eyeballs in*) and the deceleration experience at retrofire (*eyeballs out*).

fail-soft

A malfunctioning computer that continues to produce incorrect information despite its built-in shut-off mechanism.

false leap

When a futurologist makes a forecast that fails to take into account the always unpredictable human response to technological change, he is said to commit a *false leap*.

father file	Any current master file of data for a computer system.
FAX	Computer slang for any reproduced (*i.e.,* facsimile) document; also, occasionally used as a verb to describe sexual relationships with a partner other than one's spouse.
first generation	Those initial commercial computers, operated by vacuum tubes, that are no longer in use.
flopsy	A flexible storage disk for programming microcomputers. Also used by computer people to characterize their personal working areas (*e.g.,* desks). As in "Just put the coffee on my *flopsy,* please."
fox messages	Slang for the nonsense phrases employed to test computer equipment. Also used to characterize interoffice memos heavy on verbiage but light on content. The expression is derived from the old typewriter test, "The quick brown fox . . ."
freefall	A condition of being so hopelessly drunk that one is no longer in control of body movements. Adapted from the term describing the condition of weightlessness in space.
futuristics	The science of forecasting the future. *Futuristics* is currently the most popular buzzword for this discipline, but there are now other contenders to the throne, including *alleotics, futuribles, mellology,* and *stoxology.*
gang punch	Computerese for punching the identical information into all of a group of cards. Much more interesting, however, is the secondary

slang definition: an office party in which one worker (female) invites several co-workers (male) to join her in an activity that still does not—to date, at least—compute.

garbage
Buzzword used to describe either incorrect input (human error) or incorrect output (computer error). For similar reasons, computer personnel are usually referred to as *garbagemen* or the *sanitation department*.

glitch
A sudden, unexplained surge of energy in the circuits, causing a malfunction in an electronic device. Also, *glitch* can be used as a verb to characterize the mess caused by an unexpected problem.

God's engineers
Contemporary religious groups have of late employed experts in management methodology to reorganize and streamline their ecumenical structures. Industrial engineering firms that specialize in such consultant work are also often called *Missionary Control*.

going home to Ma
Ma here is a shortened version of "matrix." Many technologically rooted firms are changing their organizational structure from the more traditional, more rigid hierarchy-pyramid form to a more flexible, free-wheeling matrix.

graceful degradation
Paradoxical expression coined by technocrats to euphemistically characterize the reduction of services offered by a computer service.

growzy
Affectionate buzzword, joining *grumpy* and *drowsy,* to describe a computer that's slow in responding to instruction.

gulp   A group of bits is called a *byte*. A group of
                    bytes is called a *gulp*. Computer people seem
                    to find this uproariously funny.

hands on   This expression is used to indicate that a com-
                    puter or computer terminal isn't available be-
                    cause a programmer is using it.

hit   Can mean either the successful completion by
                    a computer of a program step, or the equally
                    successful completion of the entire program.

hitchhikers   Computer-age bandits; electronic-whiz rogues
                    who've somehow contrived to illegally plug
                    into an artificial intelligence system for per-
                    sonal gain.

housekeeping   Expression for computer operations that
                    don't contribute directly toward the problem-
                    solving but are instead designed for purposes
                    of initialization, set-ups, and mop-ups. Also
                    called *bookkeeping*.

huminals   Researchers engaged in trying to create
                    methods of contact between humans and ani-
                    mals.

illegal operation An operation the computer cannot perform
                    because it hasn't been designed to deal with
                    that particular function.

infer retrieval The process, practiced exclusively by human
                    minds, in which conclusions are reached by in-
                    ferential (that is, deductive) reasoning. Never
                    to be confused with *info retrieval*, which is the
                    computer-science method of solving problems
                    strictly on the basis of recorded information.

inhibit   Space-age phrase meaning "prohibit."

I/O   Input/Output. The briefest way to sum up the
                       human ("input") and computer ("output")
                       symbiosis.

iteration   Computer lingo for repeating an entire series
                       of instructions to the machine. The term has
                       been adapted to describe a research techno-
                       crat who is nonmechanically engaged in solv-
                       ing a problem through the old-fashioned trial-
                       and-error process. "To *iterate* is human; to
                       forgive does not program."

kaleidoscopy   An ill more and more of us are becoming heir
                       to: the condition of dislocation and alienation
                       that comes from being constantly bombarded
                       with chaotic technological changes.

KISS   The very first instruction a computer pro-
                       grammer trainee receives, *KISS* stands for
                       "Keep It Simple, Stupid."

kludge   Linguistically obscure nonsense word used by
                       technocrats as a term of endearment for a
                       computer.

life supports   Futuristics lingo, taken from space-age
                       terminology to characterize small supportive
                       groups designed to replace institutional care.
                       Thus, old-age homes would be replaced by
                       self-governing retirement centers, mental hos-
                       pitals would be replaced by at-home therapy
                       sessions, etc.

LISP   Acronym standing for List Processing; that is,
                       a computer program designed to simply
                       process all data into the form of a list. Also

employed as a sardonic reference to a human being addicted to habitual list-making. "Jones has got a real bad *LISP* problem."

liveware *Ware* is a suffix widely employed to describe various facets of computer science ("software," "hardware," etc.). *Liveware* is a tongue-in-cheek reference to computer scientists.

LSD Acronym for Least Significant Digit or immaterial computer data.

machine-sensible Specifically, any material that can be "read" by a computer. However, calling someone *machine-sensible* is a high compliment, meaning as it does a nontechnocrat nevertheless gifted with an extremely disciplined mind.

MMing Technocratic slang for "mathematical modeling," the reduction of a concrete problem into its abstract symbols in order to more easily arrive at a solution. *MMing* is the human equivalent of the basic computer process.

Memorylane Dump Fictitious place name for those sections of a computer used to store already programmed data for future reference.

metas The most currently advanced computer systems, built for use by management executives who have not necessarily been trained in artificial-intelligence science. Although easily operated, *metas* (meaning "more comprehensive") are highly sophisticated devices that function as the manager's personal assistants.

mode Indisposable technocratic buzzword supposedly limited to a definition of a specific method of performing a task ("Let's approach this in an interpretive *mode*") but often used in the sense of personal attitude ("Don't mess with Jenkins today. He's in a mean *mode.*")

modem

"Modulator-demodulator"; a *modem* can be either the linking device (usually a telephone) between the programmer and a distant computer, or the middleman passing along information from the technocrat who gathered it to the technocrat who will use it. (Nontechnically, a gossip-loving person will often be described as the *neighborhood modem.*)

Monte Carlo Night

A mathematical technique utilized only when all else fails. It's based on the same laws of averages gamblers use when calculating odds and bets. The expression is often employed to indicate that a problem cannot be solved by computer, as in "Better get ready, it's *Monte Carlo Night.*"

MVT

An acronym for Multiprogramming with a Variable number of Tasks; that is, setting up a complex set of instructions for a computer assigned to perform several functions at once. Since this often leads to error, both machine and human, it's been said that *MVT* also stands for Multiprogramming with a Vast amount of Troubles.

nerveless breakdown

Computers have reached so extreme a point of sophistication that they've been known to become "overexcited," "depressed," and— worst of all—even "illogical." The expression *nerveless breakdown* characterizes any and all computer malfunctions that cannot be traced back to simple mechanical failure.

Norman Pet name for the very newest type of forecasting method, one that is less concerned with what *might* happen than with what *should* happen. This reflects a general change within the science of futuristics; where once futurologists were concerned with predicting the future, they're now beginning to actually attempt inventing it. The word is always used as a proper noun, as in "I'm tired of our normal forecasting techniques. What do you say we check this one out with *Norman?*"

number cruncher Industry code for a computer that's been built solely for use in mathematical calculations.

numb ex Acronym standing for "numerative executive"; that is, a management or technologically oriented business person who uses his/her own minicomputerized calculator for everything from estimating a possible merger to figuring out the grocery bill.

obedient A computer that arrives at its assigned goal by performing its programmed instructions exactly is said to be *obedient*; a computer that arrives at the correct goal but bypasses or creates its own instructions is labeled a *rogue*. (As artificial intelligence systems become increasingly complex, instances in which computers reject human instructions and replace them with their own are becoming more common.)

offline Technically, *offline* is used to characterize electronic equipment that's not directly linked to the central computer system. Technocrats, however, also use the expression to describe someone who's not very intelligent and/or aware. "Bill's a nice guy, but he's a little *offline.*"

Anyone who is deemed intellectually worthy is *online*.

oily rags

Unflattering nomenclature coined by front-office technocrats to identify those colleagues who are more involved with the actual machinery. Also directed, sarcastically, against upper-echelon types who still like to get their fingernails dirty poking through the innards of their electronic charges.

OLIVER

Both an acronym—On-Line Interactive Vicarious Expediter and Responder—and a celebration of its originator, Oliver Selfridge. Depending on one's personal feelings about technology in general, this is either the most exciting or most frightening computer-system innovation to date. Briefly, OLIVER is an intensely personalized intelligence unit programmed to provide its owner with the type of information needed to make daily decisions. As a matter of fact, OLIVER can be designed to *decide* for its owner. At the moment, these decisions are still pretty minor: "What should I buy for my wife's birthday?" or "Can I afford to eat out this weekend?" Specialists predict, however, that OLIVER may shortly be able to help us choose who to vote for, or who to marry.

paper wedding gowns

Generic buzzphrase used to characterize what is seen to be among the most revolutionary of all social trends: the growing popularity of "throwaways," or deliberately short-lived and easily discardable consumer goods. Among the ever growing list of throwaway products must be included cigarette lighters, razors, and toothbrushes (which can even be bought with pre-loaded toothpaste).

peekaboo
A system in which a computer can check the accuracy of its data cards by placing one on top of the other and matching the punch-holes. Likewise, it also describes a system futurologists employ to compare all facets of a problem.

PLATO
Acronym for Programmed Logic for Automatic Teaching Operations, a standardized instructional system used throughout the country as a teacher's aide for students ranging from kindergarten through graduate-school age. Lower-cased, *plato* becomes a noun describing any computer employed for scholastic programs.

polling the room
Mission-control lingo for consulting all the technicians present before solving a problem with the spacecraft that is being monitored. Also used in a general sense for getting a general consensus before making any decision.

postmortem dump
Computerese for the area in which all mistakes, human and mechanical, are stored as reference to avoid similar future errors. A technocrat, just informed of a mistake, might very well respond, "Oh well, I'll just file it in my *postmortem dump.*"

pressure garment assembly
Originally, NASA jargon for "spacesuit"; lately, the expression has become a jocular reference to formal clothing. "Don't forget, Bill. The party's going to be strictly *pressure garment assembly.*"

problematique   Futurologists' buzzword, first used at a special U.N. meeting, that refers generally to the continuing and worldwide ecological crisis.

propars   Abbreviated form (pronounced PRO-pars) of "professional parents," that is, couples trained to act as surrogate fathers and mothers for children. *Propars* are, claim the futuristics advocates, the wave of the future.

PSZ   Yet another futurologists' code word, this one standing for Personal Stability Zone. This is a generic expression describing people's more enduring relationships—whether it be with one's family or one's favorite old pair of blue-jeans—that provide them with an anchor in an otherwise constantly changing world.

reset to zero   Technocrats' buzzphrase, drawn from computer science, for starting all over again. Less pungent substitute for "back to the old drawing board."

retrofit   Widely used buzzword describing the correction of any facet of a program while that same program is in effect.

robotics   The science of artificial intelligence systems that have been placed inside automatons. It was Czech author Karel Čapek who invented the word "robots" back in the early 1920s for his play *R.U.R.* (which stands for Rossum's Universal Robots). The work terrified audiences with its portrait of a world taken over by sexless and dispassionate machinery. That terror remains to this day.

sensible atmosphere	Untypically straightforward NASA lingo for that part of the earth's atmosphere that human beings live in.
shorties	Slang term used by futurologists and other social engineers to characterize those human relationships—one-night stands, for example—that are deliberately designed to be short-term.
shot	In computerese, that period of time in which a programmer can use the system; in other areas of life, the designated interlude two people spend together.
simplex	A communications link capable of transmitting data in only one direction, or a person who's a gifted talker but a terrible listener. In both cases, the opposite would be *duplex*.
SOB	Sonic Boom; that is, the bang caused by atmospheric shock waves when an aircraft reaches the speed of sound. A really loud *sob* has been known to shatter window glass, and so the acronym is particularly apt for those long-suffering people living directly beneath airport flight paths.
therblig	One of 18 symbols used as the basis for time-and-motion studies. Frank G. Gilbreth was the engineer who designed the symbol; *therblig* is his last name spelled almost backwards.
time	*Addtime* is the time required for a computer to perform simple mathematical processes; *availtime* is that time the computer is available for use; *connecttime* is the length of time a pro-

grammer actually uses the system; *downtime* is the length of time a computer is inoperable because of malfunction; *realtime* describes computer systems that produce data fast enough to affect an ongoing activity; *runtime* is the time the computer spends on one particular problem; *setup time* is the time between computer runs; *standby time* is the interval between asking the computer a question and receiving the answer; *turnaround time* is the interval between the computer producing the answer and the interested scientist receiving it; and *weedtime* is the time spent removing unnecessary data from the storage areas. All these terms are used by technocrats to describe the equivalent situations in their personal lives.

totaprobes
Catchall phrase for "total zones of probability," which are futuristic amusement centers in which gratification for all sensory needs will be provided. The prototypical *totaprobe* would be a hybrid of Disneyland, Asbury Park, Monte Carlo, and a Storyville whorehouse.

The Technocrats

Military Talk

accidental delivery of ordinance equipment

As in "We've just accidentally shelled our own boys." (Also called *friendly fire*.)

acute environmental reaction

Brass talk for "battle fatigue," which used to be brass talk, too, for the psychic wounds of combat. If a trooper, just relieved from a thirty-day duty tour atop a continually bombarded hilltop position, begins to tremble uncontrollably, the medics will typically give him four aspirin, 48 hours of bed rest, and a notation in his records that he's suffering from an *acute environmental reaction*.

(the) Alamo Hilton

The dug-in position along the front-line perimeter of a combat zone is usually referred to by its defenders as "the Alamo." The *Alamo Hilton*, then, is the headquarters bunker (which, also usually, has a few more creature comforts than the rank-and-file barracks). Also, *the Dodge City Hilton, the Tombstone Hilton,* and *Boot Hill*.

alphabet soup

ABC: Atomic, Biological, and Chemical warfare. As most modern-day nations have the capacity to use any one (or all three) of these, the U.S. Arms Control and Disarmament Agency (ACDA) has recently stated that "Everyone's in the soup now." ACDA has also defined biological and chemical weapons as "generally intended for disabling or destroying people, plants, or animals, rather than *real* property." (italics added)

apple

A private code word for the Marine Corps, one which will often be tattooed, either phonetically or symbolically, on an enlisted man's shoulder.

ASS
ASS stands for Arms Stability Situation, a delicately balanced neutral zone in which all sides maintain but do not increase their stockpiles of weapons.

believer
A captured enemy soldier is a *believer;* a dead enemy soldier is a *true believer.*

bug bunnies
Bug bunnies are the bacteriological scientists specializing in biological warfare. Immediately following World War II, General Eisenhower remarked that such experts were "beginning to multiply like rabbits."

burg bargaining
A strategic deterrent (already hypothesized in the novel *Fail-Safe*) that is designed to limit nuclear war. Based on the biblical injunction "an eye for an eye," the concept is to prevent a total holocaust by "only" destroying one city in response to nuclear attack. By bargaining in this manner, it is believed that the aggressor will be persuaded to control the extent of its own assault. Also known as the *Tit-for-Tat Tactical Response.*

casualties
Although not a military word *per se, casualties* has brought out so much etymological creativity in the Pentagon that it should be included here. *Friendly casualties* refers to any losses on our side. From there we go to *friendly light casualties,* which is an officialese description of losses up to 40%; next is *friendly moderate casualties,* which includes losses up to 80%; last but not least, *friendly heavy casualties,* which is 80–100%. Enemy casualties are not called *un-*

	friendly casualties but rather *enemy casualties.* All enemy casualties are always labeled *heavy.*
CEP	Circular Error Probable (pronounced "sap"); according to the 1976 SALT lexicon, "a measure of the delivery accuracy of a weapon system . . . which (always) has a .5% chance of failing."
cibber	A good soldier; a man one can trust; a competent, battle-tested veteran. The first three letters of this word are an abbreviation for the Combat Infantryman's Badge, a citation awarded to everybody who has been engaged in at least five days of continuous combat and one of the few medals taken seriously by the troops.
civilian irregular defense soldier	An extremely ornate replacement for the term "mercenary," which, according to a Pentagon handout, "has unfortunate connotations of a 'have-gun-will travel' nature." A rose by another name, the *civilian irregular defense soldier* does, nevertheless, give his services for money instead of conviction.
close, but no cigar	A somewhat less formal way of acknowledging an error, the *close, but no cigar* mission—also called the *near miss-ile*—is any nuclear device that fails to strike its intended target.
collateral damage	If a megaton bomb is dropped on a military facility or force, and if that facility or force happens to be situated in an otherwise pacific location—Chicago, for example—then the resulting destruction of "non-active personnel" and "non-active structures," *i.e.,* you and me and the homes in which we live, is referred to as *collateral damage.*

contact	In official battle reports, one never "fights" but rather makes *contact* with enemy forces. This deliberately neutral word is often used to cosmetize the black eye resulting from an unsuccessful engagement, such as a rout or an ambush.
counterinsurgency	*Counterinsurgency* is a military operation against guerrilla forces. It is often used by banana-republic dictators to disguise the fact that what's being fought is not a small rebellion but is instead a full-scale civil war. From 1963 to 1966, South Vietnam referred to its war as a *counterinsurgency mission* (for much the same purpose that the previous Korean War was described as a "police action").
credible deterrent	This is nuclear threat as a public relations ploy, an ineffective weapons system that has been so hyped that the enemy believes it to be far more devastating than any counterstrike could possibly contend with. There have been many *credible deterrents* invented over the years, one of the funniest being the dread "Le-Page gun," a mythical Nazi weapon that was supposed to shoot a ton or so of glue at Allied planes in midflight.
credible threat	The *real* thing; any weapon—offensive or defensive—that does exist and that is effective.
denying the enemy valuable resources and cover	This is a very convenient buzzphrase, much beloved by military strategists, that both describes and rationalizes wholesale slaughter via thermonuclear weapons. Destroying a missile site is *denying the enemy valuable resources and cover*; as is bombing farmland, blowing up forests, wiping out civilian cities.

derosing

An anagram for "date of estimated return from overseas," and the sweetest phrase in the enlisted man's vocabulary. "I'm *derosing*" means "I'm going home!"

develop community spirit

A leftover phrase from the Vietnam War: if an invading army enters a village, disposes of all the local leaders, summarily executes all civilians believed to be collaborators, and sets up a Vichy-type ruling class, that army credits itself with *developing community spirit*.

discreet burst

Like Alice's looking-glass, this expression reflects the exact opposite of its implied meaning. A *discreet burst* is actually several rounds of ammunition pumped into various innocent bystanders. Also, *probe, prime selection,* and *constructive load.*

disestablish

Covers everything from the voluntary closing down of a military position to the (involuntary) destruction of that position. (Big business has picked up the phrase as a convenient buzzword for dismissing an employee.)

(the) Elephant

A combat soldier quickly learns to distinguish all kinds of fear, from the brief moment of flustered nerves to the adrenaline-fueled blind panic. But when you're really frightened—that is, when your heart feels suffocated, your breath constricted, your muscles absolutely immobile—then, and only then, have you experienced *the Elephant sitting on your chest.*

expecting rain

The Pentagon code for an all-out nuclear attack, *expecting rain* is the ultimate weather report.

FF Zone   Approximately twenty years ago, the United States military instituted a plan in which certain combat areas could be designated as Free-Fire Zones, *i.e.,* zones in which soldiers were given literal license to shoot at everything that moved. Today, if a peace-time trooper says, "Lately I've been living in the *FF zone*," he means that he's going through some particularly hard times.

football   Chillingly casual slang for the metal case that contains all the codes necessary for beginning a nuclear attack. The small suitcase is carried by a military officer (the *bagman*) who ceaselessly follows the President on his daily rounds.

footwear maintenance engineer   After long, and rather expensive, debate, the Senate recently decided to change the title of "Congressional Bootblack" to the *Footwear Maintenance Engineer.* Not one of the more vital pieces of legislative action, but nevertheless, a reasonable example of the power of words to glorify any position.

frag   The word was first coined to describe an unorthodox (although highly effective) form of protest. If an officer was deemed too difficult to deal with, one of his men would point out the error of his ways by rolling a live fragmentation grenade into his tent. If the officer still failed to get the message, a second grenade—this one with its pin pulled—would arrive. Now, *fragging* is used for any (violent but rarely as murderous) action initiated against an overly hardnosed superior.

fratricide   Not, as you might reasonably expect, another way of describing nuclear war, but instead a term for an accident which occurs when too many weapons are fired too close together. If they collide and explode, they've committed *fratricide*.

fubb
It's official. The dated *snafu* (situation normal, all fouled up) has now been replaced by the equally eloquent *fubb* (fucked up beyond belief).

greenbacking
The hiring of mercenary troops is called *greenbacking* the troops. Also used as a euphemism for an under-the-table bribe, as in "You wanna get out of KP, all you gotta do is *greenback* the Mess Sergeant."

(getting our) hair mussed
Machismo appraisal of the potential damage an enemy's strike-force can inflict.

high burn rate
Specifically, a missile with its principal thrust occurring immediately after take-off is said to have a *high burn rate*; generally, a commissioned or noncommissioned officer who is very aggressive in his duties.

hostile unfriendlies
Double negative notwithstanding, this is the official term for the enemy, whomever and wherever he may be.

humane removal
Another one of those mirror-phrases so beloved by the Pentagon's p.r. department, *humane removal* is the razing of an entire village ("for strategic purposes") and the removal of all its inhabitants to a displaced-persons camp ("for their own good").

ice
"We've been *iced*" in military jargon means an ambush or frontal attack.

infrastructure	The fixed services—*i.e.,* the airfields, fuel dumps, communication and supply systems—that an armed force requires in order to properly function. This is the formal definition of *infrastructure;* the word, however, has been so used (and abused) that President Carter recently declared a cease-fire on its employment in all Defense Department-to-President memos.
jack in the box	A dead soldier being transported home in the standard GI aluminum coffin.
kill ratio	An ugly phrase that covers a variety of ugly concepts: the body count (in which commanding officers are required to match the number of enemy dead each day against a quota), the "assets-debits" list (in which the number of dead enemy is compared with the number of dead friendlies, thus allowing some armchair commander the joy of making pronouncements like "our boys are worth five of their boys, and we've got the figures to prove it!"), and the "cost-factor" account (in which it's estimated just how much money the taxpayer has to shell out for each victory). A brief amplification of this last item: At one point during the Vietnam War, a journalist pointed out to a press officer that it currently cost about $1,000 to kill one enemy soldier. The offended officer shouted back: "So what? How can anyone put a price on human life?!?"
LOW	Limited Open Warfare; that is, a conflict in which opposing sides abide by specific restraints so as to avoid escalation or a spread into neighboring territory (*cf.,* the United Na-

tions Command during the Korean War). Conversely, *HIGH* is Highly Intensive General Hostilities, or a full-scale conventional war. The next step, which is the last step, is an *all-out,* War Room lingo for nuclear combat.

lose your bubble The first crude submarines were controlled by the use of a level (similar to the ones employed by carpenters) in which the bubble's position simulated the relative position of the vessel. *To lose your bubble,* then, is to lose control of the situation and become swamped by indecision.

lurped out To be in a state of total exhaustion. *Lurp* is an acronym for Long-Range Reconnaissance Patrol, one of the most dangerous and debilitating details a soldier can pull during wartime.

MAD The unthinkable end of the unthinkable atomic crisis, and, too, the most appropriate acronym in this chapter, *MAD* is Mutually Assured Destruction.

maximum bad The very worst situation to be enmeshed in. Being taken prisoner of war is *maximum bad.*

mega A prefix for the quantity one million, widely used to describe (and not so coincidentally to reduce the impact of) various elements of the Atomic Age, *e.g.,* "megaton," "megabar," "megacycle," and "megadeath."

mixed-manned Catchy catchphrase for a military force that's composed of men from two or more nations. NATO, for example, is a *mixed-manned* outfit.

mobile maneuvering When a carefully plotted withdrawal (read: retreat) does not go according to plan, but instead disintegrates into a disorganized rout, the potential black eye may be avoided by praising the escaping troops' skill at *mobile maneuvering.*

nonessential personnel

A polite military expression for all civilians, lower-echelon soldiers, and easily replaced laborers who happen to be caught in the middle of the battle. Since they're not important to the outcome, they're not important.

nuke threshold

That point in an international conflict beyond which nuclear weapons will inevitably be brought into use. At the height of the Cuban Missile Crisis, President Kennedy alerted the armed forces that the U.S. had reached the *nuke threshold;* the next Presidential order would have been to *go nuclear,* that is, to prepare for nuclear defense of the country.

on point

In a combat patrol, the man *on point* is the advance scout; in peacetime, the man willing to take the *on-point* position is the man willing to stick his neck out for his fellows.

OOPS

Occasionless Ordered Preemptive Strike. Another apt acronym, this one referring to a war that begins accidentally rather than by design. Is such a disaster possible? Writes Herman Kahn: "Not only is the accidental thermonuclear war possible but, given the balance of power, it is the most probable cause of war in the world today."

pacification

According to most standard dictionaries, *pacification* is the process of peace-making; according to the Pentagon lexicon, however, it's the process of peace-making by first making war.

preventive war   An unintentionally ironic way to rationalize striking the first blow. The *preventive war* is a (usually) surprise attack designed to destroy a nation before it is inspired to destroy you. (Attila the Hun would have greatly appreciated this peculiar point of view.)

provocation   Any excuse for instituting a war. The excuse doesn't have to be important, indeed doesn't have to be genuine. In *The Language of Specialists,* military expert Robert Hunter suggests that the possession of inferior nuclear weapons by a nation "might be *provocative,* since, as they must be used at the start of a nuclear war in order to be effective at all, these weapons might inspire a preemptive attack."

real world   The definition here differs according to rank. For the brass, the *real world* is the military world; for the grunts, the *real world* is the civilian world. Reality, Schopenhauer once wrote, "is dependent upon the position one is standing in while perceiving it."

response   Pentagonese for a military action in response to an enemy attack. A *flexible response* is any counterattack that equals, but does not exceed, the force of the initial attack; a *controlled response* is a counterattack that is deliberately less than the initial assault; a *selective response* is stronger; a *finalizing response* is an all-out salvo designed to destroy the aggressor nation.

response to impact   Whatever is left standing (or breathing) after a nuclear siege is that target's *response to impact.* Given the capabilities of most atomic weapons, this phrase is usually amended to read: *zero response to impact.*

returnee	If an enemy soldier defects to our side, he is not a deserter but rather a *returnee;* if one of our soldiers defects to the other side, he is a traitor.
scaled	Very effective grunt word for the effects of long-term combat. "I've been *scaled*" can be translated as "I've lost every need but one—the need to stay alive at any cost."
search & clear	The Pentagon's official replacement for *search & destroy* mission. Still referred to by the troops, however, as *search & scorch*.
skunk works	Defense Department lingo for a small team of highly trained specialists assigned to one specific job. As the team is freed from the usual burdens of supervision—that is, no one is permitted to interfere with them—and as it's usually housed in a restricted area away from everybody else, the term *skunk works* has been coined to describe the specialized operation.
slicks	Newly inducted troops, so-designated because they have yet to earn either chevrons or decorations to wear on their uniforms.
software	Weapons, especially nuclear weapons, are *hardware*; the intelligence, either human or computer, controlling the weapons is called *software*. (Weapons-control rooms, incidentally, are known as *appliance stores*.)
spasm	From the Greek, "to tug." A nuclear response to a non-nuclear attack, and the stuff that nightmares are made of. The possibility of a small nation decimating its neighbor with a megaton bomb, and thus triggering the apoca-

lypse, is one of the most frightening facts of atomic life. To paraphrase T. S. Eliot, "This may be the way the world ends, not with a bang but with a *spasm*."

stability of power An unintentionally ironic way to describe the Mexican stand-off in the modern-day world, *stability of power* really means that war is unlikely because all interested parties have enough fire to collectively demolish the galaxy. There might, conceivably, be a victor in a nuclear war, but he'd have precious little ground to stand on.

strike The strategists' indispensable word for a thermonuclear attack. *Preemptive strike* is an attack deliberately initiated to forestall the enemy's attack; *preventive attack* is an attack launched against a nation before that nation has acquired enough fire power to launch an attack against you; *first-strike* is an offensive assault; *second-strike* is a retaliatory countermeasure; and *massive strike* is sending in every missile, bomb, and rocket one has on hand.

throw weight Pentagon term for the power (in megatons) of an enemy's nuclear arsenal.

unacceptable damage To the military mind, *unacceptable damage* is the amount of potential damage that could be inflicted upon an enemy and so deter him from responding in kind; to the unmilitary mind, *unacceptable damage* is any damage inflicted by any power on anyone.

4

Voices
of the
People

Voices
of the
People

Helpful Talk
High Talk
Sex Talk
Street Talk

The most vibrant of all jargon is that of the People: Street Talk, High Talk, Sex Talk, and Helpful Talk. All are far more closely tied to the ways in which ordinary folk live their lives than are the jargons of the powerful, the media, and the technocrats. In addition, and despite an initial feeling of hostility given off by the Voices of the People, their language is not only far less exclusive but actually inviting: it shows a readiness to accept all newcomers—provided, of course, that the novice is ready to share a lifestyle, whether it be on the street corner, in a drug-dominated atmosphere, a rigorous boudoir, or the California sunshine, where many of those who use Helpful Talk seem to spend much of their lives.

Helpful Talk is the jargon used by those who pursue physical, mental, and spiritual perfection through a gamut of philosophies, some as old as India and others as new as today. Perhaps a better definition can be found in their own jargon. Their key word and highest ambition is to *actualize*, and if they *do*, their *actualized* selves have realized full human potential. ("Gestalt" *used* to be a key word, and referred to the entire human organism; it has now been abandoned, however, because of rampant vulgarization.)

Inasmuch as Americans' fascination with their own heads and healths is a recent thing, so Helpful Talk is the newest of the jargons. But it also may well be the most humorless. The condition of complete adaptability, for example, used to be known as "AC/DC." Unfortunate sexual connotations, however, forced that expression to be jettisoned in favor of an acronym based on the same letters, namely *acdac*. Of course, anything directly sexual that helps one on the road to actualization can be talked about, and is, but never in such a way that pleasure *alone* is the purpose or was the result. For example, however earth-shattering a moment might have been, it is referred to in Helpful Talk as an *interaction*. The same rule applies to the description of orgies, which at their more abandoned level are known as *social interactions*, and at their more conservative, where those involved have met before, *extended-family interactions*.

Sex Talk, too, tends to be somewhat humorless, much of it reflecting the unending pursuit for partnership that takes place in the singles bars. Once inside, the man or woman of few words can pick from a variety of to-the-point one-worders: *moy*? (My place or yours?); *McQ*? (Meaningful quickie with the implied promise of something more permanent being likely); and *BC*? (Do you use birth control pills?). The pornographic movie industry has contributed its share of Sex Talk, too, including *inscrewtable* (a porn flick starring an Oriental) and *pornchops* (one that combines sex and violence).

Not unlike Sex Talk, High Talk, the jargon of the drug culture also tends to reflect the utmost seriousness with which drug users pursue their pleasures. Unlike Sex Talk and other People jargon, however, High Talk has a social progression to it, from the different ranks of dealers (*baggies*, "street dealers," to *Oz Men*, who sell to the *baggies*, to *The Kilo Connection*, who sells to the *Oz Men*) to the different ranks of *heads* (*A head, B head, C head*, etc.), each into a different drug.

Without doubt, the liveliest of all People jargon is Street Talk, the slang heard on every street in every American city. More than all other jargons it constantly adapts to changing times— and more than all others it also promises, at least on the surface, hostility to the stranger. No tough Western baddie was ever given a line that contained the degree of threat contained in "Hey, *Chuck*...," a greeting for anybody who doesn't belong on the street and who, in self-interest, had better go away, or "You better *hat up*," a warning to leave or else. Much Street Talk was originally Black in origin, even though today the sidewalks might be slightly integrated with *coal burners* (whites who socialize with Blacks). An even larger degree of integration that has taken place on urban streets in recent years is the arrival of people who speak Spanish—and that language has also added a flavorful spice to Street Talk. *Andale* (get out of here) is a Spanish equivalent of, and just as ominous as, "Hey *Chuck*." A jargon reply might be *con safos*, which at its politest translates as "the same to you." This, of course, should be used only with great caution—but then so, too, should all jargon. After all, the novice in any new language is likely to make at least some mistakes.

Voices of the People

Helpful Talk

acdac

Originally, this was *ac/dc,* but it's been recently changed to avoid the sexual connotations in the term. *Acdac* characterizes those of us capable of adapting comfortably to any situation. Also, *cosplug* (that is, plugged into the cosmos).

actualize

The essential self-help word, coined by mainstream psychologist Kurt Goldstein, describing any person (and any process) dedicated to the full realization of human potential. The completely actualized man or woman is unfettered by neuroses, has no need of artificial mood controls, and resides (as a full-time citizen, not a part-time tourist) in reality.

ahisma

Ahisma (pronounced ah-HIS-ma) is a profoundly tranquil condition in which one has achieved a loving relationship with the world. Anybody fortunate enough to reach this state may be referred to as an *ah-ah head.*

alone together

One of the basic tenets of self-help philosophy is that while we're all one with the universe, we are also finally, irrevocably, alone. Thus, marriage (with its assumptions and commitments) would appear to be an unrealistic move for actualized people. In order to solve this dilemma for those couples not wishing to be divorced from either reality or each other, the phrase *alone together* has been devised as an acceptable definition of legal wedlock.

AMORC

Abbreviation for the Ancient Mystical Order Rosae Crusis; or, less formally, the Rosacrucians. There are literally thousands of self-help sects, but this one (dating back to Lower Egypt) is the grandfather of them all. Although now pretty much reduced to recruiting disciples via the back pages of romance magazines, the influence of the Rosacrucians must never be underrated. Just stare at the rear end of the dollar bill. That pyramid-encased eye staring back at you is the AMORC symbol of eternity.

Anastenarides

A Greek ritual, still held each May, in which true believers stroll unscathed across a path of red-hot coals. Somewhat demystified during its passage to America, the rite now demonstrates one's belief in oneself. There've been other changes, too; for one thing, U.S. practitioners perform it while wearing sandals; for another, the coals have been replaced by barbecue charcoal.

apart

Slang word for a condition of confusion, or an inability to complete the process of actualization (as in "I've been involved in self-help therapy for five years, but I'm as *apart* today as I was when I started."). The opposite of *together*, although the latter slang word has now pretty much been replaced by *whole*.

ASC

Alternate State(s) of Consciousness; and what this chapter is all about. Strictly speaking, an ASC cannot be experienced through drugs, religious ecstasy, or UFO sightings. Other than these, however, just about anything goes (and often does, all the way from the now-conventional Orgone Box to the still unorthodox Creative Buzzsawing).

ashram

In India, a religious retreat; here, any simpatico group activity (including Great Books clubs, the P.T.A., and car pools).

avatar   Spiritual guide; encounter-group leader; self-help therapist. The word is that *guru* has become definitely déclassé.

be easy   Friendly admonishment to maintain a non-judgmental (*i.e.,* actualized) approach toward life; a transcendental interpretation of "stay cool, fool."

belly music   In Oriental philosophy, the stomach is widely regarded to be the center of consciousness; American mystic Edgar Cayce believed that any continual singsong could encourage the brain into its alpha state. Thus, *belly music*: any chant, prayer, or sound that relaxes the mind and frees the spirit. The most popular are the Buddhist "OM," the Tantric Yoga "Nam y'ho renge kyo," and the various TM mantras, but almost anything repeated often enough—and this includes chanting the Lord's Prayer, the Pledge of Allegiance, or your favorite college football cheer—will suffice.

big MAC   *MAC* is an acronym for "Mellow at All Costs," a mental attitude that is, times being what they are, no small achievement. Thus, a *big MAC* is someone who never loses his/her cool, regardless of the provocation.

blowout center Originally, the official name for R.D. Laing's revolutionary treatment institution, where psychotic patients were encouraged to work out their feelings of madness through shouting, temper tantrums, and infantile behavior; today, any environment to which one can retreat for emotional release. A *blowout center* can be your therapy group, a deserted stretch of beach, or the basement recreation room.

brutal	In California, *brutal* has now replaced the once ubiquitous *heavy* to describe any concept or person that is notably profound ("That Sartre is one *brutal* dude."). Only time will tell whether and for how long the word will be accepted by the rest of the country.
CARE package	CARE stands for circulation, assimilation, relaxation, and elimination—the basis for the holistic movement. "Holism" itself is an interesting term; specifically, it's the philosophy taught and practiced by groups like the Wholistic Health and Nutrition Institute; generally, however, because the holism method emphasizes the relationship between mind and body, it can refer to any actualized process of healing.
(having your) Chakra gonged	*Chakra* is a Hindu word meaning "wheel of energy"; striking gongs is a way of reaching an ASC level. "I really had my *Chakra gonged* today" simply means that you've been working and/or playing at top-efficiency level.
channels	Psychic healers, like Norbu Chen and Kathryn Kuhlman, prefer to think of themselves as *channels* through which the curative powers of actualization are transmitted. Likewise, anyone successfully treated in this manner has not been healed but has rather been *channeled* back to health.
circumpointer	Description of a self-help teacher who instructs his charges by circling around a concept without ever actually pointing directly toward it (and so allows the students to make their own discoveries).

coming into birth	Also, *re-entry; the endless beginning; turning the wheel; awakening; brief peace;* and *back to the drawing board.* Various euphemisms for dying, the emphasis here being on reincarnation. The view of death as rebirth is universal— though by no means restricted—to the self-help movement. Even so pragmatic an American as Benjamin Franklin rejected the finality of the grave; his headstone reads: "The body of Benjamin Franklin, printer, lies here, food for worms! Yet the work itself shall not be lost, for it will, as he believeth, appear once more in a new and more beautiful edition, corrected and amended by its Author...."
Corybantic dancing	Dancing yourself into abandon, ecstasy, and orgasm. One of the oldest ways to break through to the ASC experience, and still—as can be evidenced by the current disco rage— one of the most popular.
dialoguing	Speaking to each other without cant, manipulation, or fabrication. Also, R.I.P., the "meaningful rap."
edgies	Self-help buzzword for those people who have given up the comfort and security of middle-class life and who now live on the edge of all possible experiences.
ego freego	Also, sometimes, just *freego.* A condition in which one's ego has been freed from the crippling effects of insecurity. "You wouldn't go out with me if I were the last man on earth? Doesn't bother me. I'm *ego freego.*"
fadicals	Pun reserved for those self-help disciples more attracted to the movement as a fad than

as a means of achieving peace and spiritual health.

Fat City   Originally, jazz musicians' slang for the unhip and buttoned-up straight world; later, Street talk for the good life of fast cars, fast money, fast food, and fast women; now, the self-help word for a nonactualized life. If you've been accused of living in *Fat City,* don't look at your waistline—look into your soul.

fellow beings   The only enlightened way to address an assemblage of humans; as in, "Good afternoon, *fellow beings,* and welcome to our annual stockholders' meeting."

funky   It's interesting to trace the history of this particular slang word. Briefly, in the 19th-century South, it meant smelly and/or dirty; in the 1920s, it meant good (blues) music; in the Sixties, it meant anything genuine (and thus good); today, at least among self-help folks, *funky* means a sympathetic fellow traveler of the actualization movement.

gestalt   From the German *Gestalten,* or "the pattern of its parts." Once the exclusive property of Dr. Fritz Perls, a psychiatrist who devised a form of therapy that treats the entire human organism, *gestalt* has become vulgarized into a catch-all phrase meaning the whole of anything. In one L.A. restaurant, for example, an otherwise conventional menu ("Appetizers," "Entrées," etc.) has replaced the heading "Dinners" with the heading *House Gestalt*.

getting clear   In Scientology, where this phrase was first created, *getting clear* means being freed from your old self (an expensive rebirth, by the way, often costing the disciple several thousand dollars to achieve). In the rest of the self-help world, the expression is a more modest description of being freed from any neuroses or hang-ups.

go with the flow   In the Stoned Sixties, to go with the energy of whatever drug you happened to be zonked out on; in the Actualized Seventies, to go with the dictates of reality.

(the) Great Pyramid of Giza   Geographically, the house that Cheops built; spiritually, at least for the more mystical-minded self-help groups (like "Pyramid Power"), the planet earth's central source of cosmic energy.

grief work   According to self-helpers, even mourning requires a training process. *Grief work* is a series of exercises—shouting, screaming, weeping, etc.—designed to help trainees release emotional anguish when necessary.

grounding   Directing energy into self-discovery. *Grounding* has now pretty much replaced *plugging in* as the buzzword for heightened awareness.

HIQ-up   Acronym for High Incompatibility Quotient, which is considered the only ground(ing) for divorce between self-aware couples. The expression is always employed as a verb, as in "Joe and I have just *HIQ-upped*" (pronounced, by the way, hiccupped).

hyperventilation   A method of rapid breathing once believed to be excellent for meditative purposes, hyperventilation has now been discredited by self-

help therapists, who opt for a deeper, more
subdued respiration rate. The result is that
the word's been completely turned around.
"Hey, don't *hyperventilate*" is now a way of ad-
vising someone to calm down.

I hear you
Also, *I know where you're coming from.* Usually
accompanied by a sympathetic gaze and a
hand squeeze, this is an expression designed
to reassure the speaker that you understand
completely his point of view.

I'm not holding
The source of some confusion for ex-junkies
now on the actualized habit, as they once
shouted this phrase only when the narcs were
kicking in their doors at four in the morning,
I'm not holding in the self-help world may be
translated as "I'm not hearing you."

inner space
Spiritual, or self-awareness, strength. Not to
be confused with *personal space,* which is the
distance *Fat City* residents impose between
themselves and reality.

interaction
Actualized interaction is a successful sexual en-
counter; *mis-use interaction* is unsuccessful sex;
extended-family interaction is communal sex
(once known as *group grope); social interaction* is
a straightforward orgy; *secondary interaction* is
an adulterous fling; *finalizing interaction* is a
sexual connection that leads to commitment;
and *transitional interaction* is a period of self-
willed celibacy.

**Interface
Communications
System**
Not a new television network, but the old-
fashioned séance with a misleading label.

JUADing

Acronym for Jumping Up and Down. As any child can tell you, *JUADing* is a wonderful way to relieve tension, act out frustrations, and express oneness with the world. Nowadays, there's a proliferation of centers designed to free more self-conscious grown-ups from their inhibitions and turn them on to the joys of *JUAD*.

koan

Adapted from the ancient Chinese word *kung-an,* which means "legal brief," the *koan* is a story concerning the actions or conversations of any enlightenment leader. Incidents from the life of Christ are *koans,* as are anecdotes about Talmudic rabbis, the Buddha, and L. Ron Hubbard. Often apocryphal, *koans* can seem very strange to the uninitiated. One quite typical in its humor, hidden meanings, and obscure reference points, is the following:

Freud, Jung, and Adler were sitting outside one night drinking tea.

"Oh, look," said Adler, "the moon is reflected in the teapot."

"Oh, no," said Jung, "the moon is not reflected in the teapot."

Freud kicked over the teapot.

kriyas

A very spiritual word, freely adapted from the teachings of Yoga, for a less than spiritual process, the enema. "Empty your bowels," reads one West Coast colonics clinic sign, "and fill your mind."

life script

A key concept of the actualization process is to view your life as a script and to view yourself as its author. In this manner, you will dictate events rather than letting those events dictate you.

lifing

Living is merely living; *lifing*, however, is a day-by-day attempt to gain the most from existence.

love network

Thanks to advanced technology, people seeking help for a variety of problems—depression, suicidal tendencies, alcoholism, even religious crises of every faith—can now pick up a telephone and call a volunteer group of counselors trained to give both immediate advice and more long-range referrals. Also, *caring services*.

LTC

Living Together Contract; that is, a signed, sealed, and even witnessed agreement between two cohabiting adults as to who is responsible for what in the relationship. An *LTC* may be cosmic (in its definition of privacy and freedom), domestic (in its discussion of who washes and who dries), or both simultaneously. The living together contract has been adopted by self-helpers as an effective way of lowering false expectations and raising reality perception between the sexes.

MEAT

An ambiguous term, short for Me At All Times, that can be a flattering description of one's self-awareness or a less-than-flattering comment on one's plain selfishness. "You're a Grade-A *MEAT*" may be a mortal insult; then again, it may be a great compliment. When in doubt, just stay easy, keep your *ego freego*, and go with the flow. That way, either way, you can't lose.

negative positives

A highly regarded actualization technique, common to various schools, in which destructive actions are deliberately performed so as to learn from the results what to avoid doing in the future.

neutralizing toxins

Any diet or fast undergone for reasons of health and/or belief is *neutralizing* your body's *toxins*.

no deposit, no return

Buzzphrase for lowering personal expectations, which is itself a buzzphrase (credited to California's Governor Jerry Brown) describing a lifestyle that inhabits, rather than exploits, the earth. Also known, with some minor modifications, as *right-livelihood,* and *voluntary simplicity.*

nonverbal verbalizing

Popular psychology has a marked distrust of spoken language, relying instead on emotional release, the acting out of blocks, and tactile exercises to aid disciples in their journey toward the light. Even so, language is essential for communication. Thus, *nonverbal verbalizing,* a speech system in which words are used more as images than conceptual symbols.

nurturing environment

Any physical site—your analyst's couch or the local pub—that encourages feelings of peace and security.

OOBE groovy

OOBE is an abbreviation for Out Of Body Experience; groovy is one of the sole surviving slang words of the Sixties. *OOBE groovy* is an individual with a marked ability to free mind from body and soar into the upper stratosphere of cosmic awareness.

one-way tourist

An expression that both describes and condemns those members of a particular self-help group who love to watch but refuse to get involved in the often painful process of spiritual growth.

organic/synthetic Anything good for you, whether it's grown in the earth or built in a factory, is *organic;* anything bad, live or plastic, is *synthetic.*

organizing priorities I'm *organizing* my *priorities* is the only way to inform friends and strangers that you're currently engaged in self-help therapy. "I'm *re-organizing* my *priorities*" means the first self-help group you tried didn't work out so you're now trying another.

peak phreaks People who leap from one therapy group to another in a never-ending quest for bigger and more insightful highs.

positive feedback This is a euphemistic, not to mention euphoric, substitute for the word "mistake." As in "You're right, I'm wrong, secondary interaction with the milkman was definitely *positive feedback.*"

quit clicks Some people can only go so far and then no further in the exploration of self. At some point, a *quit click* is triggered—it could be having to relive a much-loved friend's death, for example, or finally being forced to come to terms with a parent—and the person finds it impossible to continue the actualization process.

real age One's spiritual, rather than chronological, age. As in: "I'm fifty, but my *real age* is five. I've been engaged in self-help for five years now."

rear-enders   Term describing any member of a T-group who specializes in surprise attacking. You've been regaling your group for the last fifteen minutes with the details of your traumatic childhood, for instance, when the person on your left suddenly breaks in with, "By the way, Mike, how's that little impotence problem of yours coming along?" No group is deemed complete without at least one psychic fender-bender.

rumpbump   First begun by the Human Potential Movement, growth games are tactile exercises (usually involving several players) designed to sharpen the body, expand the consciousness, and get in touch with the people around you. *Rumpbump* is both a generic definition of such games and a specific game, too (in which a group closes its collective eyes and rubs its collective behind).

satori   In Zen Buddhism, *satori* is the condition of absolute serenity and intuitive illumination; in self-help, it's a less permanent but no less illuminating insight.

selfless greed   *Selfless greed* is openly expressed and nonmanipulative self-interest; *selfish greed* is insensitive and driven gluttony.

shit   Thanks to Fritz Perls, we now know there are three kinds: 1) *chickenshit,* or clichéd small talk that avoids emotional contact; 2) *bullshit,* or lies; and 3) *elephant shit,* or grand plans that avoid confronting reality.

soul ax   *Ax* is an old musicians' term for instrument; a *soul ax* is any personal device—it could be singing, it could be dancing, it could be just sitting and staring into space—that satisfies the soul.

species stance

Stomach in and chest out; good posture is an important reflection of one's feelings about oneself.

stay with it

Prolonged observation. By focusing your gaze on an object, any object, and by *staying with it*, you can easily put yourself into a meditative— or at least constructively thoughtful—frame of mind.

strength bombardment

Session in which the T-group makes a verbal inventory of one selected member's weaknesses. Being told that you are, among other things, a whining, self-pitying, spineless jellyfish may not seem to be particularly helpful, but this kind of bombardment allows you to gain strength and trust. That's the theory, anyway.

structural integration

A system of deep-muscle manipulation (read: extremely painful massage) that's supposed to reduce tension and increase body awareness. *Structural integration* is simply an ASC rubdown.

Subud

One of the very newest, as of this writing, self-help therapies. It's based on no rules, no technique, no answers, and no questions. Included here for no particular reason.

tada

Hindu word that can be best translated as "Let it be." It's used to express acceptance of all things, no matter how dire they may be. ("My wife's left me, my kids have joined a commune, my dog hates me, and my house just burned down. *Tada!*")

T-group   Any kind of therapy-oriented group.

trephin   One of the earliest types of surgery was performed by tribal witch doctors who'd drill holes in their patients' skulls (to allow the devils to escape). Today, this practice still has some believers (who now, however, claim that *trephination* increases the blood to the brain, thus increasing its power). You don't have to have a hole in the head to be *trephined,* though; it's often used in contemporary circles to describe the effects of an insight, *e.g.* "Yesterday, I trephined on this childhood memory of being caught in class with my fly open."

valnew   A new actualized value (love for all things) that replaces an old nonaware value (love for all money).

Who you screaming with?   Not a cocktail-line opening when being introduced to Fay Wray, but a friendly question asked when two actualizing friends meet after a long hiatus. Primal therapy, developed by Arthur Janov, depended on patients performing repeatedly such exercises as infantile regression and infantile screaming. *"Who you screaming with?"*—which can be translated to mean "What therapy are you involved in these days?"—is a nod of the *ah-ah head* in recognition of Janov's contributions to the self-help movement as a whole.

WISH   An acronym for One World, One Spirit, One Humanity.

Voices of the People

High Talk

A-bomb

Any mixture of drugs (marijuana and hashish being a particular favorite) that's smoked, snorted, or swallowed. Such volatile combinations have been dubbed *A-bombs* partly because of the immediate euphoric rush to the brain and partly because long-term use tends to give that happy brain the consistency of sculptured cumulus.

African bush

Hashish; that is, the resin of the female cannabis plant. Also, *black Russian, chunkies,* and *hash*.

A head

In the Sixties, a *head* was anyone plugged into the counter culture; today, he or she is anyone plugged into drugs. *Head* itself is a generic term; the prefix determines the specific trip. The *A head* is into LSD (acid). The *B head* takes barbiturates. The *C head* believes things go better with cocaine. The *garbage head* gets off nondiscriminately on everything. The *hop head* jumps for joy at the sight of opium. The *juice head* loves his alcohol. The *shit head* is a heroin user. (Incidentally, this last expression is used strictly by initiates. If, for some reason, you should ever happen to be introduced socially to a junkie, never say by way of greeting: "Hiya, *shit head*, glad to meet you." This is considered bad form, and may lead to many deplorable consequences.)

aimless Amy

Slang for amyl nitrate, a stimulant often used to prolong orgasm. It is dispensed as a capsule, which can be snapped and then inhaled by both participants. Also, *pearls, poppers, posies, snappers,* and *uncle emils*.

AMA

Abbreviation for American Mind Agents, a catch-all phrase that includes all officials—judges, lawyers, politicos, police, and undercover narcs—who work for the drug enforcement system in this country. AMA in this context is also a peripheral swipe at the American Medical Association (whose policy of coming down hard on even the softest highs has subjected it to much scorn from certain quarters).

amps

Generic term for drugs, either swallowed or injected, that stimulate the central nervous system. Besides being a shortened version of amphetamines, *amps* is also a pun on the high-energy jolt taking such a drug induces. (Likewise, depressant drugs will often be called damps.) A.K.A., *bams, boosters, chaulkers, footballs, green dragons, jelly babies, jolly beans, peaches, peps, sparkle plenty, speed, sweets, truckers, ups* and/or *uppers, wake ups, whities,* and *zooms.*

angel dust

Gentle slang for a savage drug: Paraphenathrene. Legally, it's used as an animal tranquilizer; illegally, it's used as a cheap but potentially destructive high. *Angel dust,* usually sold in powder form, is a devilish concoction that can lead to severe psychotic reactions, cerebral hemorrhage, or death. Also, *fairy dust, hog, moon beams,* and *PCP.*

anywhere

This is the most current euphemism for the possession of drugs. "Are you *anywhere?*" means "Are you selling?"

artillery

Any and all paraphernalia associated with the taking of narcotics. *Light artillery* refers to soft-drug equipment like rolling paper (*skin*), roach holders (*crutches*), coke spoons, and hash pipes. *Heavy artillery—i.e.,* hard-drug equipment—is also known as *works*.

backwards Tranquilizers used to cut through a panic drug reaction and bring the user back to solid earth. *Forwards* are chemical stimulants that send one soaring again.

bad craziness Strictly noncommittal definition of actions and/or hallucinations while under the influence. An intense sexual bout is *bad craziness;* so is seeing the *crank bugs* crawl about your feet.

baggies Street dealers, so-named because they sell only small amounts of drugs (usually sealed in plastic bags). Also, *arreadors, candy men, junkers, mothers, peddlers, pushers, tambourine men, the source, thoroughbreds,* and *travel agents*.

balloons Heroin. So-termed because it is often sold in rubber balloons. In this way, it can be swallowed (when the heat comes down) and later safely excreted for use. Also, *boy, chiva, dogie, 8, H, Harry, horse, junk, lemonade, scag, shit, smack, snow, tecata,* and *the white lady*.

Barbie dolls One or more of the central-nervous-system depressants that fall into the pharmaceutical category of barbiturates. Each particular chemical preparation (Luminal, Tuinal, Seconal, etc.) has its own slang equivalent, which explains why the *B head's* vocabulary is peppered with such phrases as *reds, bluebirds, seggies, yellow jackets, King Kong Specials,* and of course, *Ken dolls*. By the way, in upper-middle-class society, *dolls* can mean any pill, whether it be a stimulant or a depressant.

blank	A container of non-narcotic substance that is sold as the real thing. Also used as a verb to describe the rip-off, as in "I tried to score an ounce of pot, but some dude *blanked* me with a baggie of oregano."
(the) Book	In *Valley of the Dolls, the Book* is holy writ. Always capitalized, its real title is the *Physicians' Desk Reference,* the annual compendium of all commercial pharmaceutical preparations.
booster shooter	A term of utter contempt reserved for addicts who engage in petty stealing, most often from supermarkets, to support their habits.
boot	Slang verb for injecting a drug intravenously. Also, *bang, fix, geeze, hit, jolt, make, pop, shoot, tom,* and *tom mix.*
bum bend	*Bad trip* is exclusively employed for acid; *bum bend* describes a journey on any other drug that has suddenly gotten out of hand. "That grass is bad medicine. It starts you out on a real scenic route, then sends you around a *bum bend* in the road."
businessman's trip	A high that lasts only two hours or so; that is, the approximate time of a business lunch.
cartoon	Hallucinating while under the influence. Always used as a verb, as in "Dropped some acid last night, and didn't stop *cartooning* till dawn."
clarabelle	Buzzword for Tetrahydrocannabinol, the active chemical compound in marijuana (often produced and sold in synthetic form). The drug probably earned this nickname because of its side effects: giggling, facial distortions,

inability to walk in a straight line, and general clownish behavior. Also, *clay, sin* (short for synthetic), *grass,* and THC.

cocktail

Remnants of a reefer, *i.e.,* the *roach,* inserted into the front end of a regular cigarette and then smoked.

contact high

There are two meanings here, one for soft and one for hard drugs. Anyone who's ever sat in a smoke-filled theatre watching a film popular with heads, like *2001* or *Star Wars,* knows how intoxicating it can be to inhale others' marijuana fumes. *Contact high* is also, however, a (somewhat sarcastic) term describing the vicarious pleasures and horrors of addiction experienced by nonuser pushers and narcs. From William Burroughs' epochal novel, *Naked Lunch:* "Selling is more of a habit than using, a *contact high,* and that's one you can't kick. Agents get it, too. Take Bradley the Buyer. Comes to look more and more like a junkie. He can't drink. He can't get it up. His teeth fall out. Fact is his body is making its own junk or equivalent."

crank bugs

The more malevolent hallucinations that come crawling out of a *bum bend,* ranging all the way from the little green men to the big pink elephants.

crankers

Otherwise straight people who need a variety of pills to get up in the morning, get through the day, and get back to sleep at night.

dope

Once an outsider's term for any narcotic substance; now an in-word for marijuana. Also—

depending upon region, lifestyle, or time warp—*baby bhang, boo, bush, charas, charge, dagga, dirt grass, duros, dynamite, gage, gangster, ganji, gauge, giggle weed, grass, griffa, gunny, hay, hemp, herb, iceberg, icepack, jive, joy smoke, juanita, leno, loco, love blow, M, margarita, marjorie, mary ann, mary jane, mary warner, mary weaver, michoacan, the mighty mezz*, MJ, *moocah, mota, mutha, pod, pot, rainy day woman, rama, red, rough stuff, stum, sweet lucy, T, tea, 13, tosca, yedo,* and *yesca.*

do-rights

Reliable dealers are called *do-rights,* after a popular television cartoon character. Unreliable dealers are called, depending on their relative size, anything you can get away with.

fix

A word defining both the jolt from narcotics use and the obsession with drugs of any kind. "The people who walk the streets, the people who work every day, the people who worry so much about the next dollar, the next new coat, the chlorophyll addicts, the aspirin addicts, the vitamin addicts, those people are *fixed* worse than me. Worse than me. *Fixed.*" (From Jack Gelber's play, *The Connection*.)

flush 'n' mush

Coded warning to get rid of one's drug supply immediately (to avoid arrest, prevent seizure, or anticipate a parental visit). *Flush* because drugs at home can best be disposed of down the toilet; *mush* because, if stopped on the street or in a car, the only solution is to gobble down the drugs on the spot.

geronimo

Liquor that's been spiked with barbiturates. So-named because indulging in this Molotovtype cocktail is about as safe as jumping from an airplane with a Kleenex parachute.

groovers

The only form of *groovy* still in common use, *groovers* are teenagers into "kiddy kicks," *i.e.,* sniffing glue, drinking soda pop laced with aspirin, inhaling nail-polish remover, etc.

honeymoon

Junkie word for that period of time when he/she can still get high from heroin. Eventually, the narcotic will be needed to maintain a (relatively) normal state of being.

hooter

Cocaine, cocaine, keeps running through the brain. A.K.A., *Bernice, blower, Charlie, coke, flake, girlfriend, happy dust, initiative, Lady,* and *star stuff.*

hot turkey

Unconventional way of smoking dope by first igniting the entire joint and then inhaling the resultant fumes. The term's a pun on the expression *cold turkey.*

housewife's delight

Tranquilizers, like Valium and Librium, usually taken (or so rumor has it) by bored, discontented suburban women.

ice in (your) shoes

A derogatory term directed at one who is fearful of trying a new drug. "Hey, there's nothing wrong with this stuff, I mean, the zoo uses it to calm down the bull elephants in heat, I mean, what's your problem, you got *ice in your shoes?*"

in the power

"Jack's *in the power*" means Jack's selling good drugs.

(a) Jefferson airplane

A match split down the middle and used to hold the remnants of a joint so as to smoke or

inhale it. The acid-rock band The Jefferson
Airplane (now The Jefferson Starship) named
itself after this makeshift roach clip.

jones   This word is used both to describe a narcotics
habit and the cold-turkey withdrawal from
that habit. There are two possible sources for
the rather odd term: a pun on the old cliché,
"Keeping up with the Joneses"; or a derivation
of "jakes," a 1920s Southern colloquialism for
the peripheral neuritis caused by bad corn
liquor.

joypop   An injection of a drug subcutaneously rather
than intravenously (the latter is known as
mainlining).

**kicking
the habit on the
elevator**
This expression describes the long-term,
stage-by-stage withdrawal from one of the
most pervasive, most addictive, and most dangerous of all drugs: nicotine. There are two
puns at play here: the first can be found in the
process itself, a slow descent away from the
cigarette fix; the second can be found in the
"No Smoking" signs now hanging in many ele-
vators courtesy of legislative mandate.

(the) Life   The daily routine of a head, including scoring,
using, and interacting with other heads. (The
opposite is *on the natch* [natural], a lower-cased
life without drug-induced highs, fantasies, or
connections.)

lines   Drugs in powdered form—cocaine, for instance—are chopped up with a razor and then
laid out on a mirror in thin lines that are
snorted through a straw or spoon or a rolled-
up currency bill.

long cut	An irresistibly compelling need for food, usually junk food, that occurs after smoking several joints over a short period of time. Although not one of the main horrors of the *Life,* the munchies can be a bummer when it's three o'clock in the morning, the refrigerator is bare, the nearest deli is two miles away, it's raining outside, and you've got a craving for Twinkies that just won't quit.
mash Allah	Arabic for "gift from God"; opium. This still popular phrase dates all the way back to the 17th century, when it was coined by nomadic Tartars who used opium to replenish not only themselves but their horses, too, over long journeys. Also, *black stuff, can, Chinese tobacco, cubes, dream, hope, ice cream, mud, O, oye,* and *tar.*
merk	This word, code for the best-quality drugs (whether they be heroin, grass, or alcohol) has been created in honor of Merck Sharp & Dohme, a pharmaceuticals company highly regarded for the superiority of their products.
mesmerizing sight	A painted dot, symbol of the mystical "third eye," that is worn on the foreheads of the more deeply involved—or more deeply out of it—*A heads.*
Mighty Joe Young	If a drug user has a habit, he's carrying a *monkey on his back;* if it's a heavy habit, he's got *an ape sitting on his neck;* if it's a killer habit, he's periodically subjected to *Mighty Joe Young crapping on his brain.*
mike	Standard drug talk for one microgram (that is, one millionth of a gram).

(on the) nod

Slang expression for someone who has just mainlined heroin. It comes from the general drowsy condition of a junkie, in which the head, shoulders, and upper body move up and down in a continual nodding motion.

OJ

Abbreviation for Over Jolt, meaning a too-large dosage of hard narcotics. Since the police and hospitals commonly use the expression OD (Overdose), *OJ* has been created as the heads' alternative so as not to identify them with the official establishment. (A similar expression, *OA*—or Over Amp—is used to identify the hallucinating state caused by a too-large dosage of Methedrine.)

owsley

The very best LSD, the *crème de la crème* of acid, so-termed to commemorate Augustus Owsley, grandson of a Kentucky senator, who arrived in Haight-Ashbury in 1967, spent the next two years cooking up the most potent hallucinogenics in San Francisco, and then disappeared as mysteriously as he came. Because of the by-now mythical connotations of the name, *owsley* is also sometimes used to describe any splendid experience.

(the) OZ Man

The second-tier distributor on the marijuana milk-train. *The Kilo Connection* buys the grass in large quantity, and sells it to *The Oz Man*, who cuts it into pounds and ounces, and sells it again to various dealers working the streets.

pass go

A successful drug transaction is known, after the "Monopoly" board game, as a *pass-go*. An unsuccessful drug transaction? Do not pass go. Do not collect two hundred dollars. Go directly to jail.

pellet	Currently the most common slang word for LSD. Also, *A, acido, the big Chief, the big D, blue cheer, cresto, dome, instant Zen, L, pink swirl, sugar, tric, 25, wedge,* and *white lightning.*
pinhead	A miserly, thin joint—the exact opposite of a *firecracker*—the *pinhead* goes up in smoke as soon as it's lit.
pins 'n' needles	Morphine. Also, *aunt emma, M, miss emma, mojo, morphie,* and *white stuff.*
poison people	Head slang for heroin and methadone addicts, low men on the highs totem pole.
potlikker	A tea made by boiling marijuana *lumber, i.e.,* the leftover twigs and seeds, that reputedly gives the drinkers a fair-to-middling high. Prior to the 1930s, when grass was declared a "dangerous narcotic," this brew was called *poppy tea,* and could be bought at the neighborhood apothecary.
put in writing	Sending drugs through the U.S. mails is a tried-and-true method of distribution. There's a wide variety of ways to do this, from simply hollowing out a few tomes and sending them "book rate," to elaborately saturating a postcard with soluble chemicals, limited only by native imagination and jail-shy discretion. The one cardinal rule: Never put a return address on the package.
Q	Abbreviation for Quality. There is an incredibly long list of quality types for each drug. Marijuana, to cite just one, has over 100 "brand" names, each with its own place on the rating system. Among the most familiar are

Acapulco gold, Colombian green, and Panamanian red (all rated excellent); Canadian black, Chicago black, and Congo dirt (all very good); Mexican brown (okay); Texas tea (fair); and Jersey hemp (terrible). Latest on the scene, and the most potent—and expensive—to date, is the self-descriptive Maui Wowee.

Q & Q
Abbreviation for Quantity. "How much Q & Q you looking for?" is dealers' lingo for "How much drugs do you want to buy?" Staying with marijuana, units of measurement break down as follows: *nickel bag* (1/4 ounce); *dime bag* (1/2 ounce); *lid* or *oz* (1 ounce: this last, by the way, pronounced the same way Dorothy pronounced it); *brick* (1 pound); and *kee* (2.2 pounds).

quill
Folded matchbook cover, soda straw, spoon, or rolled paper money bill used to inhale powdered drugs. (See *lines.*) Incidentally, the inhaling itself is called *raring.*

reader
A prescription obtained from an unscrupulous doctor *(hungry croaker)* for otherwise illegal narcotics.

righteous bush
Part of the ritual involved in blowing grass is to inhale deeply, exhale slowly, close your eyes in appreciation, and say "Wow. This is *righteous bush.*"

scrubwoman's kick
Naphtha is a liquid hydrocarbon solution that puts off intoxicating fumes (producing dizziness, loss of muscular coordination, and a mild euphoria).

short go	Buying a lesser amount of drugs than represented is a *short go*. Also, *short count, short piece, short weight,* and *I want my money back.*
sneeze it out	"I'm trying to *sneeze it out*" means "I'm in the process of breaking my drug habit."
steamboat	Yet another way to inhale marijuana, this time by punching a hole in a cardboard toilet-paper roll, sticking the joint through it, enclosing one end of the roll in your hand, and breathing in the fumes through the other. This method—which both traps and cools the smoke—is employed only by diehard potheads who don't care about the impression they're making (not good) on the others in the room.
ten-cent pistol	In the lower circles of the junkie inferno, strychnine is often sold as heroin (the poison looks and tastes like the real thing). A *ten-cent pistol* is a ten-dollar bag of the stuff, more than enough to put the addict into no-reentry-possible orbit. Also, *hot shot.*
throw (me) out	Plea for gratis drugs, as in "It's been a dry week, man. How about *throwing me out?*"
toss out	Con game in which a junkie visits a doctor and pretends to be suffering extreme withdrawal symptoms in order to promote both sympathy and a prescription for the drug in question.
White Light	The ultimate high for *A heads,* a condition in which the brain feels suffused with luminous light, usually accompanied by a feeling of omniscience. Also, *clear light,* and *owsley power.*

Voices of the People

Sex
Talk

AFT time

Acronym for After Two (Drinks). Within the last decade, that urban phenomenon known as the singles bar has evolved into a total subculture, complete with its own modes of dress, behavior, and (mostly coded) language. It also has several basic "laws," one of which is that a woman accepting a second drink from a man is actually accepting an invitation to spend the night with him.

argees

That is, RG's; that is, Real Girls; homosexual jargon for women who enjoy the company of gay men, the *real girl* nomenclature distinguishing them from the transvestites who aren't really girls. Also, *queen bees* and *fag hags*.

ballroom

A singles bar noted for the sexual availability of its patrons. *Make-believe ballroom* is a singles bar that has the style but not the substance (*i.e.,* willing bedmates) of a good pick-up spot.

BC

Birth Control. "Are you *A D* or *B C* ?" means "Are you using a birth control method, or am I risking a paternity suit?" *A D* stands for Accidental Daddy.

bicycle

Bisexual. Previously, the more explicit *bi* was the code word for a person who enjoys both sexes, but there's no point in a code that everyone—initiated and uninterested alike—understands. *Bicycle,* on the other hand, is so successfully obscure that a song celebrating the joys of bisexual sex, "I Want To Ride My Bicycle" (recorded by the rock group, Queen) made the 1978 Top-Ten list without offending even Anita Bryant.

buttered bun   *Bun* is one of the many buzzwords for wife or girlfriend, and not to be confused with *buns,* which is slang for buttocks. The full expression was first coined by wife-swappers; if a man is making love to his mate, and if she's already been with several other lovers the same evening, then that man enjoys his *bun buttered*.

(the) cannibal   Has recently begun to replace the ever-popular "69" as a description of mutual oral sex. Hardly the most tender of love words, it's mainly used in jest: "Like the man once said, the worst *cannibal* ever given was excellent!"

catcher   Homosexual argot for a man taking the passive role during coitus. *Pitcher* is the man taking the aggressive role. *Switchhitter* is the man taking either role.

chicken hawk   An adult gay male who is attracted to young boys.

chubby chasers   Men and/or women with an itch for Rubenesque lovers. Even in the aggressively sexual world of modern-day Don and Donna Juans, *chubby chasers* are famous for their cunning and fierce determination; they stalk Weight Watchers meetings, fat farms, and the dessert aisles of local supermarkets for their plump prey.

connecting   Singles-bar buzzword that serves as a euphemism for a pick-up, actual sexual intercourse, a more lasting relationship, and/or a little late-night conversation before going home alone.

culture(s)   Depending on what's preceding it, this indicates the specific sexual pleasure being sought. *English culture* refers to either bondage or S&M. *French culture* calls for oral sex. *Greek culture* is sodomy. *Roman culture* means orgies.

dabble A woman who only occasionally prostitutes herself (also known as a *suburban special*).

eroduction Industry name for erotic movies, a clever but not yet widely accepted replacement for *skinflicks, sleazeteases, wet movies,* and (seen on a Columbus, Ohio, theater marquee) *lewdytunes.*

gentleman Another code word that can be found in sex ads. If, for instance, you should ever happen to see something like this:
"Warm and gentle but vivacious blonde lady, 25, looking for action, wants interested and mature *gentleman* for fun and games."
in your newspaper, be warned that *gentleman* (usually, but not always, preceded by a word like "stable," "mature," or—most obvious—"generous") is a clear signal that the lady's services will not come free of charge.

governess A woman skilled in the ways of sexual bondage and domination. Often used in sex ads, porno book and film titles, and personal conversation to indicate a penchant for S&M. Also, *dominatrix, maitresse,* and *Mom.*

hankypanky In the old days, this was a euphemism for any type of sexual activity; in these new days, however, it refers to the gay male cruiser who informs interested passersby of his sexual tastes via a handerchief (or sometimes a set of keys) dangling from his back pocket. The handkerchief itself signals homosexuality; its color, and also the pocket from which it hangs, indicates the particular act its owner fancies.

heteromessual   Aggrieved gay population's code word for the straight—often oppressively straight—world.

hipsies   Sexual surrogates, both male and female, employed by therapists to help alleviate their patient's hangups. *Hipsies* is taken from IPSA (International Professional Surrogate Association), which trains and certifies all professional sex instructors.

hobosexual   Person who delights in jumping from one bed (and one partner) to another.

hot cross buns   A married heterosexual male indulging in homosexual activities. *Hot* is a long-time buzzword for sexual arousal; *cross* is a straight person crossing over the gay sexual borderline; *buns,* as noted before, is a euphemism for buttocks.

HUMP   The official U.S. prostitutes' union. Built along the lines of more conventional labor unions, it boasts several nationwide chapters, a large dues-paying membership, and its own monthly magazine. *HUMP,* incidentally, is an acronym for "Hookers United Mostly for Profit."

inscrewtble   Industry name for any pornographic film that features Oriental women.

junior birdmen   A not-very-secret secret club, its roots extending back to various ivy-league college fraternities, dedicated to the "sex as scorecard" approach. The club's full name is "The Up And

Away Junior Birdmen For A Hornier America Association." Members can be easily identified by the miniature wings they sport on jacket pockets. White wings mean the wearer has had sexual relations with only white women; an additional set of black wings means he's been with Black women; yellow wings are for Asian women; pink wings are for genital sex; pink wings worn upside down are for oral sex; red wings are for intercourse with a woman during her menstrual period; and broken wings are for sex with a man.

Kansas yummies Term for young women too naive or too innocent (or too smart) to be taken in by the usual male seduction methods.

kiki One of the most prevalent male myths regarding lesbians is that all homosexual women can be typed as either "butch" (that is, masculine) or "femme" (that is, feminine). Lesbians, correctly pointing out that they—like everyone else—have both male and female characteristics, prefer to think of themselves as *kiki* (that is, "kind of this, and kind of that").

leather lounges Pick-up bars patronized by homosexual men who like to emphasize masculinity by dressing in such macho outfits as motorcycle jackets, studded pants, heavy boots, etc. *Leather lounges* often, although not always, attract gay males who are into S&M.

lewdies An acronym, of sorts, for Let-out-for-the-Evening Wives. Many couples who practice open-marriage techniques allow each other one night a week, no questions asked, for sexual experimentation. *Lewdie* is singles-bar talk for a married woman looking for a one-night stand.

McQ   Meaningful Quickie; that is, a brief sexual en-counter that may eventually lead to something a bit more profound.

milk cows   The more exclusive brothels hire women whose only job is to examine the clients' penises for possible venereal disease. The less elaborate houses require the prostitutes them-selves to perform this service. Either way, the examiners are known within the profession as *milk cows*.

Minnesota Strip   An expression first coined by New York City police to identify the haunts of streetwalkers (many of the young women had been re-cruited straight off the buses from locales such as Minnesota); now a description used by most large cities for the area where prostitutes tend to gather most. *Minnesota Strip* has pretty much replaced the older expressions, *red-light district* and *the tenderloin*.

moy   Singles-bar acronym for "My place or yours?"

ones   Still another single-bar acronym, this time standing for One-Night Experiences. "I don't know what the problem is, but every guy I've been meeting lately is only good for *ones*." (Many bars, incidentally, will include the word "ones" in their name to serve as a signal for on-the-prowl singles.)

orbit   Once strictly a prostitutes' buzzword, now a general slang word describing sex that includes oral-genital copulation. Also, *around the world, half and half,* and *moon shot* (when anal-oral sex is part of the love-play).

player   Pimp. Also, *daddy, easy rider, low rider,* and *mack.*

pornchops   Industry name for films that combine sex and violence in one package.

retreads   Recently divorced people back on the highway of singles life.

rough trade   Homosexual lingo for young men who sell themselves to older men, but who are hetero-sexual in personal preference.

scheme-ons   Opening lines; that is, the various (calculated) approaches involved in picking someone up. Some of the very worst *scheme-ons* include: "What's your sign?" "Do you come here often?" "Why don't you smile?" "Haven't we met before?" "Is this your first time here?" "What's a foxy lady like you doing here all alone?" (this last line usually delivered to a woman who's sitting with several female friends), and "How about a little kiss, baby?"

scram scam   One of the most common con games. The hustler (male) stations his confederate (female) on a street corner. Then he selects a likely looking sucker and asks if he'd like to sample the wares. If the mark agrees, the hustler signals to the woman, who then walks into a nearby building. "Wait fifteen minutes, and go to Apartment C," says the hustler, collecting the fee. By the time the John gets to the door, the two con artists have disappeared.

sextechs

Men and women skilled in love-making techniques but not in emotional commitment.

tearoom trade

Male homosexual expression for gay men who give and receive anonymous sex in public bathrooms *(tearooms).*

train

Several orgasms, one after the other, with the same woman. Never to be confused with *pulling a train,* which is several men, one after the other, with the same woman.

TV

Abbreviation for transvestite; that is, a person who achieves sexual gratification by dressing in the clothes of the opposite sex. Other terms for male *TV*'s include *cross dresser, Mister Sister,* and the *NQ (Not Quite) Queen.*

upper frontal superstructure

Sex therapists' professional vocabulary is strictly nonsexual: for instance, female breasts are referred to as the *upper frontal superstructure.*

urbanonymous

Word created by sociologists to describe the often isolated life of the typical big-city single.

zap-in

Exchange code for your standard orgy.

Voices of the People

Street
Talk

ACT	An abbreviation for "At the Center of Things," meaning the very essence of one's life. It's invariably used in the sense of personal rehabilitation, as in "Times have been stone hard, but now I'm getting my *ACT* to-*gether*." Also, *"getting (my) shit together."*
ace	Friend. In the South, where the phrase was born, it's *ace boon coon*—an exclusively Black term. But since Street talk is used by all colors, and since *coon* still has strong bigotry overtones, and since, too, rule one of Street life is that discretion's always the better part of valor, the expression's been wisely shortened to its present form.
ace in	The verb variation is not nearly as friendly as its noun counterpart. *Ace in* means to manipulate oneself into another's situation, for money or fun or both. As in "Invited Bob's old lady back to my place for a drink last night. Now I'm *aced into* their marriage."
AD	Drug addict. The initials have been reversed to avoid confusion with *D A* (District Attorney).
ándale	An expression taken from Spanish that can mean either agreement with a proposed plan or a strong suggestion to leave the vicinity ("*Ándale*, Chuck, you're not welcome here"). Also *ódale*.
apart	Badly confused; a chaotic situation. "This scene ain't nothing but *apart*, Jack."
backdoor man	In early 20th-century blues, he was a married woman's lover; today, he's anyone who can get

	around the rules—a term of affectionate respect.
bad talk	Revolution—any revolution—from the overthrowing of a government to a dormitory food fight.
bato	Mexico City slang, now often heard on North American streets, for a tough yet honorable man. A *bato loco* is a man so tough he's foolhardy. The female equivalent of a *bato* is an *esa*.
bear	Slang noun describing something very difficult or dangerous that must be taken care of nevertheless. Also, not as commonly, used to describe a notably homely woman.
be in a high place	Happy; contented; stoned. "Scored Tuesday night. Come Wednesday morning and I was *in a high place,* man."
border	Street talk for living dangerously; a life on the very edge of death, or madness, or prison. As in "I've had it with chump dues, man. I'm moving to the *border.*"
breaking out into assholes	Great terror; as in "Was he scared? Man, he *broke out into assholes* and shit himself to death."
bro'	Short for brother; comrade. The one essential Street password. Also, *blood.*
brocas	Spanish for a real profit; big bucks; a windfall. *Brocas* has now pretty much replaced *bread.* Also, *cactus, dust, ends,* and *lace.*
burn coal	Verb characterizing a white Street person who habitually hangs out with Blacks ("Billy's sure

been *burning some coal* lately"). Reverse the order, and you get *coal burner,* a noun describing the same black and white socializing.

busting balls Several meanings are contained within, depending on just *whose* balls are being busted: "I *busted my balls*" means working too hard; "I *busted his balls*" means beating up, or overworking, someone else; "I *busted her balls,*" or more often *nuts,* means strenuous lovemaking. Also, *busting ass, busting chops, busting conk,* and *busting it up.*

busting suds Working as a dishwasher, the working world's pits. Also, though it's somewhat archaic now, *bubble dancing.*

cage High school; "Sheeeet, bro', you still trapped in the *cage?*"

call A challenge; a confrontation. As in "Better stay out of sight, man. Harry the Beast is fixing to *call* you."

case A trick word that's been used so many different ways no one is exactly sure anymore how to define it. The most scholarly source, Hermese Roberts' *The Third Ear,* gives the following explanation: "An imaginary region of the mind in which is centered one's vulnerable points, eccentricities, and sensitivities; *e.g.,* Don't get on my *case!* "

chuck Anyone who doesn't belong on the Street—a grave insult. Also, *Charlie, citizen, gray, herbie, Mickey* (Mickey Mouse), *paddy,* and *The Man.*

chump change	Wages. The not-too-subtle implication is that anyone who works a 9–5 straight job is a fool.
cojones	From the Spanish word for "testicles"; courage that's been tested under fire. "That dude's got *cojones*." Also, *balls, Hair,* and *juice*.
con safos	Derived from the Spanish, this expression can mean either "Nothing you say can hurt me" or "The same to you." Gangs will often write *c/s* on a street wall; this roughly translates into "Anything written here that insults us will bounce back and stick to the attackers."
cracker	Any bigot, white or black, southern or northern. Also, *neck,* and *peckerwood*.
crib	Home; sanctuary; a place of refuge; the neighborhood in which one lives. As in "You crazy, chump? I'm not boosting Mac's deli. That's my own *crib,* man." Also, occasionally, *crow's nest*.
cuff	Stand up. "This is the last time that bitch *cuffs* me."
cut a huss	Do someone a favor; help someone out of a jam.
deb	Female gang member. The word is a parody of debutante; in gang parlance, when a girl "comes out," she is initiated into the ranks by engaging in intercourse with each male member. (Originally, *debs* were recruited to carry concealed weapons to a fight site.)

don't meth around	Punny warning not to mess with amphetamines, particularly Methedrine. The expression replaces the Sixties slogan *Speed kills*.
feel a draft	Coded warning that a non-Street person is approaching. "Be cool, man, I'm *feeling a* definite *draft*."
flam	To be very aggressively flirtatious; usually by a male in reference to a female, as in "See that fox by the bar? Watch me put the *flam* on her."
game	To lie; to cheat; to manipulate; to avoid the issue; to be overly defensive. Always used as a verb ("Don't *game* me, Jack.").
get down	To reach into the core of one's soul; to get to the very essence of an event. "Did you see me dancing last night? I *got down,* Jack."
go upside (my) head	Literally, a hard blow to any part of the body delivered as reprimand or punishment; the phrase, however, is almost always used in a humorous, even affectionate, manner. "My daddy is sure going to *go upside my head* when I get home to-*night*."
hat up	A warning to leave—or else. "You better *hat up,* man, while you still got a head to put it on."
hawk	A crisp, long blast of wind. Named in honor of Coleman Hawkins, a great tenor saxophonist, whose music was compared to "the heartbreaking winter winds that sweep Chicago streets."
Heavyweight Jones	Nickname used to single out any con artist or street hustler—a pusher, say, or a pimp—who

is dealing with particularly dangerous scams in which the victim stands to lose a great deal more than just some money.

hit on
To make a request for anything, from a cigarette to some sex. "Got lucky last night. *Hit on* a lady, and damn if she didn't *hit on* back."

H N
House Nigger. A contemptuous reference to any bro' who's sold out to *The Man*.

hustlers don't call showdowns
Street talk translation of the old axiom: Beggars can't be choosers.

I'm whipping
Translation: "I'm doing really good, Jack, and I'm gonna do better yet."

ink
Cheap wine.

(my) jaws are tight
A warning: "Watch out. I'm really angry now."

keg
Verb meaning to pay attention. "You don't want a new hole in your face, man, you better start *kegging* me."

kite
A letter smuggled into prison. Also, *kite express*.

later
Old-time jazz musicians' salutation meaning, "So long. See you in a while." Now used as an adverb—"I'm *later,* man"—to describe the departure itself. Also, *blow, cut, jam, parking up, sliding, split,* and *taking the walk.*

light
Untrustworthy (usually more from a lack of intelligence than a lack of morals). "Don't depend on that dude for nothing. He is *light.*"

low rent	Anyone without grace or spirit. The phrase has nothing to do with money. Scrawled graffiti discovered outside a welfare office: "The people are Rockefellers; the Rockefellers are *low rent.*"
make it	In the straight world, *making it* means diligently working toward success. The Street's attitude toward this activity is reflected by its own definition of *making it,* which means removing oneself from the immediate scene.
mammy	The ultimate. "That dude's so rich he's got money's *mammy.*"
man	Initially, this was a Black form of mutual address to counter the degradation of being called "boy" by whites. Nowadays, it's a strictly neutral way of greeting another person. There's no emotional context in the word itself; one can just as easily say "How you doing, glad to see you, looking good, *man*" as "*Man,* I'm going to bust your head open." When capitalized, *The Man* means the law or any potentially repressive authority. Also, *main man,* which describes a close friend.
mira	From the Spanish word for "Look!" Generally, it means "Listen here . . ."
mother	*Mother* (which is really short for *motherfucker*) can be either a friendly form of greeting or a coded invitation to fight. The word's meaning mostly depends on whether the word's user is smiling or not—and even this isn't always the most accurate gauge. (Generally pronounced as "Mutha.")

natch trip	High accomplished by the ingestion of "natural" *(i.e.,* legal) substances, such as catnip, deodorant pads, lettuce, millet seeds, etc.
once is cool twice is queer	This is a literal—well, almost literal—translation of Voltaire's famous aphorism: "Once a philosopher, twice a pervert." Basically, it's a cherished Street principle: you can experience anything once without fear of commitment.
originals	That is, clothes that have never been washed. The expression was first used by bikers like the Hell's Angels, who pride themselves on their generally unsavory appearance.
pava	Derived from the Spanish, the word usually means playing hooky (but can also refer to the ditching of any responsibility). Also, *pinta.*
poppa stoppa	An old woman who's still sexually active.
que pasa?	"What's happening?" Once the primary form of greeting, it's been coopted by popular culture, so the Spanish version has been brought in as a replacement.
reckless eyeballing	Flirting with a person already spoken for. "Hey, fool, you been doing some *reckless eyeballing* with my old lady lately."
riff	A digression (noun); the insertion of a nonrelevant topic into the conversation (verb). The term can be traced back to musician slang for an instrumental solo.
Rig City	Any area—or period of time—where unemployment is rampant. *Rig* is short for rigor mortis.

rolling buzz	Brief euphoric feeling that has not been induced by narcotics, as in "Dancing with that woman always gives me a *rolling buzz*."
run it down	To tell the entire truth. "Don't hit on me with jive, my man; *run it down*."
same ol' same ol'	Daily grind; routine events. *"Que pasa,* Billy?" "Not a damn thing, Willy. Just the *same ol' same ol'.*"
saying something	Nonverbal but very effective communication. A man watching a good-looking woman walking sling-hipped down the street, for instance, might say: "She is really *saying something,* bro'."
short	A car, particularly a souped-up and chopped-down car. Also, *can, duby, sheen,* and *wheels.*
shuck	To string someone along; to continually fool someone. Also, *bullshit, con, jive, loose mouth,* and *small change.*
signify	To brag; to boast; to strut your stuff. *Signifying* is done more through action than talk, as in driving through your old neighborhood in an El Dorado. The word can also be employed as a putdown: "You ain't doing nothing but *signifying,* Jack."
sound	On the Street, *sound* is a verb replacement for "question," as in "Let me *sound* you on that, bro'." Among street gangs, the word describes a heavily ritualistic process of accelerating insults until they lead to physical combat.
(the) Street	A place more spiritual than geographical. *Street* is always capitalized.

thumbtripper	Expressive slang for a hitchhiker; also employed to describe someone who lives without attachments, belongings, or any close relationships. "Don't get hung up on that chick, man. She's a genuine *thumbtripper.*"
turn out	To introduce someone to something, particularly drugs or prostitution. As in "That man's one *Heavyweight Jones.* That's the third chick he's *turned out* this week."
UYA	Up Your Ass; that is, "fuck you." The abbreviated form allows one to return an insult with a certain amount of discretion (just in case the dude's even badder than he looks).
weave	To dodge out of harm's way. "Yeah, *The Man* tried to snatch me, but I put the *weave* on him."
X'd out	A once important person who has lost all his authority.
your own bad self	A very flattering way of referring to someone who's accomplished a skillful piece of work. "No jive, bro', you wrote that story all by *your own bad self* ?"
wail	A verb that can mean either being particularly adroit at some activity ("That guy can sure *wail* with a deck of cards") or to have a good time ("Me and Nancy *wailed* last night").
walk soft	To be quiet but strong: "Don't mess with me, *chuck.* I may *walk soft* but I hit hard."